Heart of Gold,
The Musical

Come on,

Come on

to the Porcupine...

Where the streets are paved with gold!

Book, Lyrics and Melodies Copyright © 2011 by Laureen Kuhl

Music, Melodies and Orchestration Copyright © 2011 by Luc Martin

Heart of Gold, The Musical is published by **Possibility Press**. email: possibilitypress@gmail.com

All rights reserved. Except for brief passages quoted in newspaper, magazine, radio or television or internet reviews, no part of this book may be reproduced in any form or by any means, electronic or mechanical, including photocopying or recording, or by an information storage and retrieval system, without permission in writing from the authors. To receive information about amateur and professional production rights, contact **Possibility Press** at the above address.

Professionals and amateurs are hereby warned that this material, being fully protected under the Copyright Laws of Canada and all other countries of The Copyright Union, and is subject to royalty. Rights to produce, film, or record, in whole or in part, in any medium or any language, by any group, amateur or professional, are retained by the authors.

Heart of Gold, The Musical was originally produced by The Timmins Symphony Orchestra, in partnership with Take Two Theatre and the Timmins Museum: National Exhibition Centre.

Cover illustration by Joel Kuhl

Interior Photos courtesy of the Timmins Museum: National Exhibition Centre

All rights reserved.

ISBN-13: 978-0-9866716-1-6

DEDICATION

For my family who have always supported me
through my worst and my best.
For the people of the Porcupine, whose courage and
tenacity embody the strength of the Canadian Spirit.
May your story never be forgotten.

Finally, for my husband who has been there at every
stage of this project, encouraging me with open
arms.

"Time may change our lives completely,
Closing every open door.
Bring on every changing moment,
Love, I would not ask for more."

ACKNOWLEDGMENTS

The size and scope of a historically based musical like this requires an equally knowledgeable group of people for an author to draw from. This musical was certainly no exception and I am thankful to each person for their contribution.

To Matthew Jones, for believing in the project from the beginning, for finding life for the project in the middle and for helping to create what it was in the end. Your commitment and love for the Symphony, Music and the City of Timmins was part of the inspiration for this project. I will always be grateful.

To the Timmins Symphony Orchestra and Chorus for seeing the possibilities of this project and being willing to give the time, effort and support that was needed to see this musical through. A special thank you to LouAnn Visconti and Luc Maisonneuve for your hard work on the production committee.

To Take Two Theatre for always seeing the joy in theatre and value in a project like this, and for offering help whenever I asked. To the Timmins Museum and Karen Bachmann in particular, for helping me with the research, giving me access to inspiring photos, transcripts from those who survived the fire, and a range of expertise. Our city is lucky to have such a dedicated team of historians.

To those who helped with my research along the way: To Anne-Elise Sauve-Jones and Luc Martin for their help with all the French phrases in the play. You made me look smarter than I am and I hope one day to speak French with a quarter of the skill you have displayed with my language.

To Helen Yaschyshyn for helping me write the Ukrainian section, saving me from translation disasters such as "Our family is on fire!" instead of "Our family's hearts are warm." And for keeping me sane by insisting that I come for a visit. You are a good friend.

To Viola and Ron Mattinen and Viola Seppa for your help with the Finnish translation and pronunciation. What a beautiful language. Thank you so much for giving me your time and knowledge and offering nice hot tea.

To the family of Pastor Ad Schwidder who graciously gave me insight to the history of a beloved family member. I hope I have brought his memory the honor it deserves.

To the Ojibway and Cree Cultural Centre for all the information on Maggie Buffalo. When I saw the big, fat file on her life I nearly cried! What a treasure.

To Dr. Cooper and Chris Bronson who gave me the Ojibway translation. What a beautiful language.

To the Timmins Public Library helping me through history files and clippings on early camp days and the fire. And for large amounts of hand-holding with the microfiche system.

To Helen and David Yashchyshyn for loaning me the letters of a Ukrainian miner from the time of the fire.

To Mert Lake for allowing me to interview you.

To the following authors and books who helped me find my way through this story: "Gold in the Porcupine" by Michael Barnes, "Pioneer Ventures: The Story of Will Bannerman in the Porcupine" by Valerie MacNabb, "The Gold Crusades" by Douglas Fetherling, "Killer in the Bush" by Michael Barnes, "Veins of Gold: 100 Years of Mining in the Porcupine Camp" by Karen Bachmann, "The Common Service Book of the Lutheran Church," "Great Canadian Disasters," by Frank Lasky.

To Kim Cogar, for all your legal help. You are a credit to your profession. And I agree with your son, you would make an excellent sidekick for Batman.

To Nancy Mattys for willingly reading my draft and giving excellent suggestions on the re-writes. Your input was invaluable. Thank you so much!

To Natalie Picard - Cavalieri for creating the beautiful dances that complement and expand this work. You bring so much skill, care and persistence to the table it has been a pleasure to work with you.

To Luc Martin, for hearing the music in my words and for finding a way to collaborate without dividing lines. What you do is amazing.

To my family and friends, especially my husband, who have supported me through this project; thank you for listening, listening, and listening, and reading, reading, and then reading again. Your honesty, interest, and kindness kept me going forward. Your sacrifices and help gave me the time I needed to get this done. I can't thank you enough.

Heart of Gold, The Musical

Book, Lyrics and Melodies by Laureen Kuhl
Music, Melodies and Orchestration by Luc Martin

Heart of Gold,

The Musical

First presented on June 7, 2012. Produced by the Timmins Symphony Orchestra in partnership with Take Two Theatre and Timmins Museum: National Exhibition Centre, and sponsored by Goldcorp, the Ontario Arts Council, Ontario Cultural Attractions Fund, The Government of Ontario and the City of Timmins.

Original Cast and Creative Team

Book, Lyrics and Melodies	Laureen Kuhl	*Music, Melodies and Orchestration*	Luc Martin
Director	Laureen Kuhl	*Music Direction*	Matthew Jones
Conductor	Matthew Jones	*Choreography*	Natalie Picard-Cavalieri
Stage Manager	Mollie King		
Set Design	Linda Jenkin	*Costume Design*	Ashley Lenartowych
Props Design	Marlies Sauvé, Sonny Newton, Kelly Killins, Jennifer Lee	*Lighting Design*	Marc Breton
André LeRoux	Thomas Vezina	*Caroline Mayben-Flowers*	Catarina Ciccone
Will Bannerman	Gordon King	*Maggie Buffalo*	Madison MacIvor-Kirkpatrick
Pearl Crawford O'Day/Charlie O'Day	Nadia Dagenais and Katie Kirkpatrick	*John Campsall*	Diego Ciccone
Frank Harson	Mits Takayesu	*Robert Weiss*	Paul Charette and Carston Skeries
John Gualey Reid	Randy Pickering	*Jeanna Weiss/ Mrs. Campsall*	Aileen Kleinhaus and Julie Verville
Pastor Ad Schwidder	Peter Davis	*Lillian Knapp*	Alison Tilley Kirkpatrick
Mrs. O'Day	Jennifer Brunet	*Christie Bannerman*	Rebecca Lord-Rainville
Minnie	Geneviève Sulatycky	*Gertrude Haas*	Emma Groulx
Rudi Puera	Patrick Pegg	*Mr. O'Day*	John Copeland
J.R. Andrews	Riley Dickson		

Chorus

Anne Marie Garon

Anne-Elise Sauvé-Jones

Bronte Cadeau

Chris Bronson

Cynthia Larche

Daryl Firlotte

Emma Tremblay

Fran Zimmerman

Irène Pépin

Jocelyn Kuhl

John Hartt

Kaileigh Vernon

Karine Mainville

Karlie Maki

Katrine Larche

Kristiina Fréchette

Laura Bronson

Lindley Morrison

Louis-Pierre Sauvé

Marlies Sauvé

Mary Lou Cameron

Maureen Favretto

Nancy Guillemette

Peggy Bendell

Shirley LeBlanc

C.W. "Sonny" Newton

Tanya Huggard

Dancers

Alexandra Lacourse

Allison Chin

Amanda Sabourin

Caleb Robinson-Ethier

Candis Blakeley

Carina Lyrette

Courtney Marcacinni-Brousseau

Cristy Webb

Daryk Richards

Emilé Fogal

Emilie-Ann Lalonde

Emma Lacourse

Gabrielle Ferraro

Hannah Whitehead

Kari Ethier

Karissa Loregio

Kaitlyn Groulx

Katlyn Harkins

Kayla Krznaric

Mélanie Veilleux

Noemie Howey-Deshaies

Rhéanne LaBarre

Sydney Legacy

Valerie Paquette

Musical Numbers
Act One

The Cultures Arrive	Will, André and Company
By the Seat of Your Pants	André, Will, J.R. and John Gualey
It's Just Like A Man	André, Caroline
The River Knows	Maggie, Caroline and Company
Come On, Come On	Pearl, John, Pastor Schwidder and Company
The Drugstore Party	Robert, Frank, JR and Company
Lillian Explains Love	Lillian, André and Company
Weiss Lullaby/Love Song	Robert, Jeanna
Through Lakes and Trees	Pearl, John
Race for the Plot	André, Caroline, Maggie, Will, Pastor Schwidder and Company

Act Two

Through Lakes and Trees	Pearl, John
Caroline's Concert	Caroline, André
Teach Me	Caroline, André
Come On, Come On (Frank's Version)	Frank
Thank God for Mothers	Mrs. Campsall, Mrs. O'Day, Maggie, Pearl and John
Frank's Song (Gold Runs in Rivers)	Frank
Fire Sequence	Caroline, André, Maggie, Will, Mrs. O'Day, Mrs. Campsall, Jeanna, Robert, Company
So It Is	Pastor Schwidder, John Gualey, Company
Caroline Finds André	Caroline, André
Love Song Reprise	Caroline, André
The Cultures Unite	André, Caroline, Christy, Company
We Are Home	Company

Cast

André LeRoux - Poor French boy from the Montreal docks with big dreams. Age: 20-30 (tenor)

Caroline Mayben Flowers - Concert Pianist from New York City. Age: 20-30 (soprano)

Maggie Buffalo (LeClair) - Ojibway (Chippewa) trapper who also works as a guide. Age: 43 at the time of the fire (soprano)

Will Bannerman - One of the first prospectors to come to the camp. Jolly Scotsman. Age 27 at the time of the fire. (tenor/baritone)

The following characters are also members of the Chorus:

Pearl Crawford O'Day - 12 years old. A very clever bookworm. (child)

John Campsall - 14 years old. Mischievous. Excels at getting into trouble.(child)

Frank Harson - Perceived by some as dim-witted, Frank is anything but.
Age: Who knows, he'd lie about it anyway. (tenor/baritone)

Robert Weiss - Champion Pie eater and well loved manager of the Dome mine.
Age: 40-50 (tenor/baritone)

John Gualey Reid - Friendly, kindhearted drifter. Age: 40+ (tenor/baritone)

Pastor Ad Schwidder - Tall, lean handsome man. He had black hair and a medium complexion. A good natured Pastor, fresh out of the seminary. Age: 20-30 (tenor/baritone)

Lillian Knapp - Local camp cook, also works out of the drugstore. Very efficient. Often seen with a cigarette hanging out of her mouth. She is hard with a soft centre. Age: 50+ (alto)

J.R.Andrews - Came north the year before. Lives at boarding house on Queen St. and kind of prospects, when he feels like it. Loves a good joke. Age: 25 at the time of the fire (tenor/baritone)

Mrs. Abigal Campsall - Worn out mother to John Campsall and several other children (three girls and two more boys) Age: 30+ (alto/soprano)

Mrs.O'Day - Mother to Pearl and Charlie. Sweet natured immigrant from Ireland. Age: 30+ (alto/soprano)

Jeanna Weiss - Finnish wife of Robert. Age: mid 30+ (soprano)

Christie Bannerman - New wife of Will (they married April 28th, 1911) Age: 25 (small singing part)

Minnie - Tough, yet pretty girl. Age: 30s (chorus singing only)

Rudi Puera - Friend of John Campsall. Family came from royalty. Age: 14 (chorus singing only)

Gertrude Haas - Friend of John Campsall. Tom Boy. Age: 14 (chorus singing only)

Mr.O'Day - Pearl and Charlie's Father. Irish immigrant, runs halfway houses and contracts on roads etc. Age: 30+ (chorus singing only)

Charlie O'Day - about 16 years old, Pearl's Brother. (chorus singing only)

Chorus (SATB)

Dancers

Act One

ACT I

1 **EXT. GOLD FIELD/MEMORY WORLD - THE CULTURES ARRIVE - OPENING**

> A cold, lonely wind blows through the hills surrounding the Porcupine Camp. Time passes, the lights shift, but the forest (represented by dancer "trees") remains quiet and still.
>
> The year is 1911. Will Bannerman, a young, jovial, dependable man, who has a moustache and wears his hat on the back of his head, walks in alone. He scans the ground for gold. Reaching centre stage he scuffs the ground with his boot in frustration. The ground under his feet turns gold. He sings.

WILL
HOPE OF ALL THE LIVING,
VANQUISHER OF STRIFE,
BRING A NEW TOMORROW,
PROMISE ME NEW LIFE.
GOLD!

> Will "stakes" his claim, by "driving" a large wooden post into the ground. His actions look and feel like an ancient ritual, "This land is mine!" He then proceeds to mark out his territory as... André LeRoux, a young, honest French Canadian with a dreamy look in his eye, enters. Even though his accent is from the poor area of Montreal, André is clearly intelligent and carries a gentleman under his rough exterior. He wanders hopefully to the stage as though he has travelled a long way. (For a translation of the following languages please see the glossary at the back of the book.)

CHORUS
GOLD! GOLD!

ANDRÉ
SOUS MES PIEDS UNE GRANDE RICHESSE.
SOUS MES PIEDS MA LIBERTE.

SOUS MES PIEDS J'EN SORTORAI,
L'OR ET LA VIE TANT REVER.

> André is joined by more French people as they joyfully look for gold on the stage.

FRENCH
SOUS MES PIEDS UNE GRANDE RICHESSE.
SOUS MES PIEDS MA LIBERTE.
SOUS MES PIEDS J'EN SORTORAI,
L'OR ET LA VIE TANT REVER.

> Other people begin to enter, singing their own cultural anthems, wearing items of clothing that identify their nationality. They carry good sized spikes (for prospecting purposes) with their flag painted on it. More people begin to join in, miners, prospectors, men, women and children from different cultures in the world: Finnish, Ukrainian, German, English, French, Welsh, African-American, Italian, Polish, Australian, Chinese ... the list goes on. Many people groups were part of this gold rush and as many as possible should be included in these parts. For these people it was a chance to change their future. A chance, unknown before the gold rushes of that time period, to change their lives and status forever.
>
> Each of the cultures arrive at the stage and stake their claim with their spike. As they do the lights turn gold. The music increases in tension. It is clear that each group, and each individual in that group, only wants gold for themselves. They will all attempt to spike the same plot of land.

ALL
BRIGHTER THAN SUMMER DAYS LOST OR WON.
BE YOU A KING OR A PRODIGAL SON,
SOON AS YOU FIND IT CONSIDER IT SOLD.
NOTHING IS FINER OR RICHER THAN GOLD.
TEASE ME NOT, TEASE ME NOT,
PLEASE BE CAUGHT, PLEASE BE CAUGHT.
YOU'LL BE MINE!
TAKE ALL I HAVE BUT DON'T LEAVE ME BEHIND.

FINNISH
KULTA!
MINUN KOTIMAA, KAUNIS SUOMI,
SUOMISSA ON JÄRIVÄ, JA JOKIA.
TOIVOTON NAHDA TEIDAT KESALLA KUN KUKKAT KUKKI.
TUON KAIKI KULLAN MITÄ VOIN KANTTA
KUN PÄÄSEN KOTIA EN LAHDEN ENÄÄ POIS.

ALL
FLAKE AND BLOCK,
CHIP AND ROCK,
MOLTEN OR COLD.
BLEAK OR FAIR,
LOST OR BARE,
COME TO ME GOLD.

GLINT AND SPARK,
DUST IN DARK,
MUCKED OUT OR TOLD.
LOAD OR PILE
WORTH YOUR WHILE.
COME TO ME GOLD.

UKRANIAN
KOLI YA PREY-DU DO-DOH-MOO,
MI ZOO-STRI-NE-MO NA POL-EEV.
TEH-PLOH NA-SHA SEEM-YA
MI BOOD-EH-MOH ZNAH-TI ZNOH-VOO.

SLAVA UCRYEENA, MOI-EE BRA-TI!
NASHI PRE-KRA-SNOO POL-EEV
ZJI-VI EEZ ZOH-LOH-TEH ZER-NO!

TAHN-TSAUE-AY, MOI SEH-STRI!
MI BOOD-EH-MOH ZNAH-TI BAH-HOT-STVO ZNOH-VOO!

KOLI YA PREY-DU DO-DOH-MOO,
MI ZOO-STRI-NE-MO NA POL-EEV.
TEH-PLOH NA-SHA SEEM-YA
MI BOOD-EH-MOH ZNAH-TI ZNOH-VOO.

ALL
KNOT AND GRAIN,
CLEFT AND VEIN,
POWER OF OLD.

SUN AND STAR,
RICH BY FAR!
COME TO ME GOLD.

SCRATCH AND KALE,
HOLY GRAIL,
BARTERED OR SOLD.
SILT OR CLAY,
MAKE MY DAY.
COME TO ME GOLD.

SCOTTISH

WHEN I WAS HAME,
A PENNILESS SELF WAS ALL THAT I HALD.
WITH A SOUGH, A CLUNK, A JILLET, AYE-O.
NOW I HEAR GOLD,
IT CALLS TO ME, "COME LAD MAKE ME YOUR OWN.
YOU'LL BE A LAIRD, A CHIEF, A KING OF AULD!"

COME YE LADS,
SAIR UP ALL YOUR MEALS ON GREAT GOLDEN SPOONS!
COME YE LADS,
IT'S EASY AS WALKING AROUND A ROOM,
OR WHISTLING A TUNE.

I'LL BE AS RICH AS EVER A LADDIE WAS KNOWN TO BE,
WITH A GREE, HA' FOLK, A HADDIN AYE-O!
AND MY OWN KIN
IN SCOTLAND WILL LIVE HIGH AND MANORLY,
WITH A CLINK, A COG, ALL GENTY MANLY WHERE EVER I GO.

IRISH

FROM THE SEA, FROM THE GLEN,
TRUE SONS OF IRELAND,
COME WE THE BLUSH OF OUR FAIR NATIVE LAND.

STRONG WE THE HEART, WE THE SOUL
OF A PEOPLE WHO
FIGHT FOR THE RIGHT OF OUR LIVES IN OUR HANDS.

COME YE PRINCE, COME YE GALE,
WORSE YOU ARE WE'LL NOT QUAIL.
WE'LL BE THE BREAK THAT ALL ILL CRASH UP ON!

    THOUGH WE BE FAR AWAY,
    HERE IN OUR HEARTS YOU'LL STAY,
    WARMED BY THE VOICE THAT DOES CALL TO YOU TRUE.

    SOON WE'LL BE HOME AGAIN,
    POCKETS SWELL ROUND THE GLEN,
    KEEP WARM THE HEARTH 'TIL MYSELF COME TO YOU.

> The golden light increases with each spike until the last group accidentally knocks over another group's spike. One of the leaders grabs the shirt collar of another. A fight is about to break out. Everyone freezes as the music rises. Slowly the scene starts to change as one by one people unfreeze and begin to "build" the Porcupine Camp.

2   **EXT. PORCUPINE CAMP MAIN STREET - IN THE TOWN**

> The shops of main street Porcupine take shape in front of the wild hills. The last two people to unfreeze (the leaders who were about to fight) make their way off stage, passed by others who are making their way into town to do business.
>
> It is morning, July 10th 1911, the day before the great fire. It is already unbearably hot.
>
> Lillian Knapp, an aged, tough camp cook with a cigarette hanging out of her mouth, shakes out a rug from the local "drug store"/blind pig. She barely appears to move and yet she is able to get a lot done.
>
> The town begins to slowly fill with people and signs of life.

3   **EXT. PORCUPINE CAMP MAIN STREET - ROBERT WEISS AT THE RAILWAY STATION**

> Robert Weiss enters, he is a large jovial man (proud winner of several pie-eating contests) and well liked by everyone he meets. He looks tired and very hot but wanders over to Lillian. People begin to head off to work or home.

> Frank Harson, a weasly, sour man with sharp eyes, sits on a bench near a wall, waiting, chewing his tobacco. He is briefly teased by the boys lead by John Campsall. Robert Weiss shakes his head at them and they stop.
>
> Robert Weiss, looking fairly tired, leans up against a post.

ROBERT WEISS

Morning Lillian. Have you heard the latest news in the Porcupine Camp?

LILLIAN

Ha! The day's hot, the bugs are biting and cold soup is on the menu. I'm not starting that stove today, so don't ask.

ROBERT WEISS

Never mind the stove. The big news today is not the weather.

LILLIAN

Why, what have you heard?

ROBERT WEISS

Oh, I didn't just hear it, I saw it... there was a fight last night, right outside my house.

LILLIAN

Again? Who was it this time?

ROBERT WEISS

Some Ukrainians and an Irishman. Ariel woke up crying again and I knew for sure a fight was going on. I threw open the curtains just in time to watch the Irishman jump on the back of the biggest Ukranian, boxing his ear as he leapt. For a little red head that was pretty impressive. But then the shortest Ukranian, a skinny one with a crazy colourful hat, snuck up from behind and hammer punched the Irishman's ribs. By the time I made it to the street there were bruises and black eyes all around. The Irishman got the worst of it, of course. I can't say he didn't deserve it. It turns out, he started the fight! What was he thinking? Three strong miners against his hot mouth and his little fist. It's a good thing those Ukrainians have some sense, or else the kid would be dead.

> Lillian shakes her head.

LILLIAN
Girl trouble?

ROBERT WEISS
Of course not.

LILLIAN
People are so crazy for gold, they've lost their minds. I hate this business.

ROBERT WEISS
Yet, here we are.

LILLIAN
Here we are.

ROBERT WEISS
The worst of it is, I'm not sure they knew what the fight was about. The Ukrainians hardly speak three words of English between them. And the Irish kid... what is it those Irish speak again?

LILLIAN
Galic.

ROBERT WEISS
Yah, well, his English is filled with it. They probably only have one word in common.

ROBERT AND LILLIAN
Gold.

LILLIAN
It's enough.

ROBERT WEISS
It's hard enough getting everyone to work together at the mine. This heat is just going to ruin everything.

LILLIAN
If it doesn't the fires will.

ROBERT WEISS
I agree with that. The last time was too close for my comfort. We barely made it down the mine shaft.

LILLIAN
Hmmm. You should look into one of those reservoirs that Mr.Meeks built. His men at the Dome did a fine job of it.

ROBERT WEISS
I'll see if I can find a crew this weekend. Can't be too careful, this weather breeds fire.

FRANK
Bring it on. We could use a good fire. It'll get rid of the chickens.

ROBERT WEISS
And how are you Frank? How is the assaying business?

FRANK
Good, good. (Rubbing his hands together) Had some nice pieces of gold through my office the other day. It's a rich land I tell you, rich!

> Lillian and Robert laugh at his enthusiasm.

FRANK (cont'd)
Ha, ha. Laugh if you want to. I'm going to get a line on some gold very soon, you'll see. I'll be out of this God forsaken land soon enough.

> Lillian and Robert exchange glances, shaking their heads. Frank is a hopeless case.

LILLIAN
Picking things up from the train?

> Frank's voice comes out in a squeak.

FRANK
Yes. I mean yes. Weights and measures, new stake documents, a plum pudding and four pairs of long underwear from my ma.

LILLIAN
You can never have too much long underwear Frank!

ROBERT WEISS
Especially in 40 degree heat.

FRANK
Ha, ha. Very funny. How would you like it if I talked about your mother?

ROBERT WEISS
Now Frank we're just having some fun. Well, I'm off for some breakfast. Salt pork and beans this morning, Lillian?

LILLIAN
No pork, but some nice fish just brought in. (Sighs) It's morning, I suppose a log on the stove is not going to kill me. The usual? Or a little liquid refreshment on the side?

ROBERT WEISS
Oh, I think both are in order. What do you say Frank? Want to take a poor little blind piggy for a walk this morning?

FRANK
Oh, I will, I will! I'd fancy a drink!

LILLIAN
Now Frank, keep your mouth together. It does far too much flapping on its own.

ROBERT WEISS
It's alright Lillian, he doesn't mean any harm. Come on by when you're ready Frank. Oh, Frank, I'm expecting some new men this morning on the train. Italians, I think. If the train comes in while I'm at breakfast, would you direct the Italians to me?

FRANK
Yeah, sure. Unless it gets so hot the town burns down.

> Robert Weiss goes inside the drug store with Lillian. Frank waves goodbye to him and waits for the train.

4 **EXT. PORCUPINE CAMP MAIN STREET - ANDRÉ AND WILL MAKE A PLAN**

> André LeRoux enters. He is looking at a map with his buddy, Will Bannerman.

ANDRÉ
So, you think there's gold on that hill?

WILL
Yes, the quartz load looks just right. George and I went over it last week. But we're all out of our stakes and claims for this year so we need someone else to buy in. It's as close to a sure thing as we can get.

André slaps Will on the shoulder.

ANDRÉ
And you would know. What do you want from me?

WILL
I need your word that you'll stake it yourself and cut us in on the money you make.

ANDRÉ
Depend on me. You and I, we'll go down to the assay office and sign the papers.

WILL
No, no, a handshake is good enough for me. There's been some funny business at the assay office lately. Charlie Savoy brought his samples in from his claim the other day, you know the one up past the lake? He was told by Frank that it was worthless.

ANDRÉ
Him? He should have known better than to take it to Frank Harson. There are smarter nuts that have fallen off trees.

WILL
I'm not so sure. I told Charlie not to sell but he was desperate to go home. Next thing you know his land is snapped up and boom, there's a real find. You know it could have been a bad sample, but I just have a feeling ... I'd rather not risk it. I trust you André.

ANDRÉ
You are bon ami, Will. Donne-moi la main.

WILL
What are you going to do with all that money?

ANDRÉ
Oh, this and that. There are trains now that go faster than a bird can fly. You know that? Even small tracks, in the city. Subways is their name.
(MORE)

ANDRé (cont'd)
They are in New York and they have them in France, soon they will be all over. Will, the world's changing and I want to be the Conductor that drives that change.

WILL
I thought you were a brakeman?

ANDRÉ
Was a brakeman, Will, was. I couldn't afford to move up. But with a little money they won't see me as a poor french garçon from Montreal, they'll see a man of distinction. This gold will be my ticket out of here.

WILL
I wish you all the best André. I never thought I would be saying this to a Frenchman but I sure will be sorry to see you get on that train.

ANDRÉ
You're a good friend Will, even if you are a Scot!

They laugh as if at an old joke.

André (cont'd)
To our partnership. To gold, et la fortune.

WILL
To gold. And a life with a new stove for Christie.

ANDRÉ
To the gold and adventure my friend, and this time a fair share in the profits, yes?

5   **EXT. PORCUPINE CAMP MAIN STREET - THE GUYS REVEAL MINNIE'S PLAN**

They pass by John Gualey Reid who is polishing a horse saddle. J.R. Andréws is with him, lazing about, chewing a piece of long grass. J.R. sees André.

J.R.
Look John, here comes André now. Hey André!

André quickly slips the map into his pocket.

ANDRÉ
Hello J.R., John Gualey, how's the horse and cart business today?

JOHN GUALEY
Just fine, thanks for asking. It's an easy morning this morning. I'm taking a load of food supplies up to the Dome from the train.

J.R.
My dear André, how is Minnie? Seen her lately?

ANDRÉ
Qui? Oh, Minnie. Oui, I saw her last night. She won't be here this morning though, she said she had to do laundry.

J.R.
That right?

WILL
Listen André, Minnie's a nice girl but I doubt she's going to be interested in the life of a train man.

J.R.
What Will is trying to say is, Minnie's not an *adventurous* kind of girl. In fact, the only adventure she's interested in is getting lost in the Eaton's wedding catalogue down at the drug store.

ANDRÉ
No! We're just friends! She likes trains and we have the same interests...

JOHN GUALEY
Wow, what you don't know about women, André, is a lot.

WILL
I thought you liked her, André. You always bring her over to visit.

ANDRÉ
Ça tourne pas rond la dedans! Because she asks to come! Aren't Christie and her good friends?

WILL
Well... Christie didn't know her well before you came along.

ANDRÉ
Tu parles! Why didn't anyone tell me?

                         WILL
You know Minnie's mom once knocked out a wrestler. Minnie's got
a better arm too.

                       JOHN GUALEY
She'll do laundry alright. She'll put him through the wringer.

                         ANDRÉ
All I told her is that I didn't want to get married... to anyone.

                       JOHN GUALEY
Oh, he's a bright one.

                         ANDRÉ
It was the truth.

                                    André starts to sing.

6   **EXT. PORCUPINE CAMP MAIN STREET - BY THE SEAT OF YOUR PANTS - SONG**

                         ANDRÉ
I TOLD HER LAST NIGHT BY THE RIVER
THE BEST THING TO BE WAS FREE

                       André (speaking) (cont'd)
and she agreed with me.

                       JOHN GUALEY
I'm sure she did.

                         WILL
How'd that go?

                                    J.R., Will and John Gauley tease André.

                    J.R., WILL AND JOHN GUALEY
OH! I AGREE!

                         ANDRÉ
THE WIND WHISTLES PAST THE GREAT NORTHERN TREES
DOWN WHERE THE PORCUPINE FLOWS.
SO CLATTERS MY TRAIN, CONTENT TO BE FREE
HOME AND A HEART SHE FOREGOES.
IT SOFTLY,

                    J.R., WILL AND JOHN GUALEY
IT SOFTLY,

                    ANDRÉ
IT SWEETLY,

                    J.R., WILL AND JOHN GUALEY
IT SWEETLY,

                    ANDRÉ
IT CALLS TO ME PLEASE
AND I FOLLOW IT WHERE 'ERE IT GOES.

                    WILL
Oh, come on André. We all know Minnie doesn't pay attention to your trains.

                    J.R.
No way! She was probably thinking something like this...

> J.R. ties a handkerchief over his head like a shawl and pretends to be Minnie. André is annoyed.

                    J.R. (Cont'd) (cont'd)
I HEARD THE WIND AND IT CALLED TO ME,
IT SAID OH MINNIE MINE,
THERE'S LESSONS LEARNED FROM NATURE
AND I SEE THAT IT IS TIME.
EVERY BIRD HAS ITS MATE,
LITTLE BEES DON'T STOP TO DATE,
I KNOW WHERE TO CONSECRATE!
WE'LL LIVE BY THE SHORE OF THE PORCUPINE RIVER,
IN A HOUSE THAT'S VERY REFINED.

                    ANDRÉ
You know we're not dating, right Minnie?

                    J.R.
I know that. It's not what you'd call conventional courting.

                    ANDRÉ
Courting?

                    J.R.
We have so much in common André... like... our interests.

ANDRÉ
Our interests?

J.R.
Yes, go on.

ANDRÉ
I LOVE THE TRAIN'S CALL ON THE NIGHT WIND,
IT CALLS ME, AND SETS MY SOUL FREE

J.R.
OH, I AGREE.

ANDRÉ
WHEN YOU STAND ALONE ON PORCUPINE HILL
FACING THE STARS IN THE SKY,
THE TRAIN WHISTLE BLOWS, THE DARK NIGHT GROWS STILL,
WATCHING YOUR WORRIES GO BY.
YOU'RE DREAMING,

J.R.
YOU'RE DREAMING.

ANDRÉ
HEART BEATING,

J.R.
HEART BEATING.

ANDRÉ
YOUR WORRIES GO BY,
WITH THE TRAIN AND THE STARS IN YOUR EYES.

JOHN GUALEY
Stars in your eyes? The last thing a woman would think about alone, under the stars is a train. With all that poetic nonsense, I'll bet she started dreaming her own dreams, the kind with white lace and a priest.

ANDRÉ
No!

JOHN GUALEY
Let an old dog show you.

> John Gualey takes out his handkerchief and ties it on his head. It's his turn to be Minnie.

JOHN GUALEY (cont'd)
MY HEART'S BEATING FAST, AND I'M OFF THE GROUND
JUST LIKE OUR FIRST DANCE.
THE GIRLS ALL STOOD AND WATCHED YOU,
IN THOSE BUSHWACKER PANTS.
IT IS CLEAR YOU SHOULD BE MINE,
IN NO TIME YOU WILL BE FINE,
OTHER GIRLS GET OUT OF LINE!
WE'LL LIVE BY THE SHORE OF THE PORCUPINE RIVER,
IN A HOUSE THAT'S VERY REFINED.

ANDRÉ
You are acting very strange tonight Minnie.

JOHN GUALEY
Oh really? I hadn't noticed. It *is* a strange night though, isn't it? So... beautiful.

ANDRÉ
Yeah, I guess.

JOHN GUALEY
It's the perfect night for... romance.

ANDRÉ
THE BEST THING ABOUT YOU MINNIE
IS HOW WELL YOU LISTEN TO ME...

JOHN GUALEY
OH, I AGREE!

ANDRÉ
I LIKE YOU A LOT, WE'LL ALWAYS BE FRIENDS,
I'LL CHERISH THESE DAYS BY YOUR SIDE.
BUT I'M A TRAIN MAN, I'VE GOT TO BE FREE,
THAT'S HOW I KNOW I'M ALIVE.
SO SADLY,

JOHN GUALEY
SO SADLY.

ANDRÉ
REGRETFULLY,

JOHN GUALEY
REGRETFULLY.

ANDRÉ
CAN'T STAY BY YOUR SIDE, BUT YOU'LL STILL BE A GOOD FRIEND OF MINE.

WILL
Oh André, you poor deluded boy. It would take more than that to dissuade Minnie. Let me lay it out for you, simple and clear.

> Will takes out his handkerchief, he pretends to be Minnie.

WILL (cont'd)
SOME PEOPLE SAY YOU SHOULD MARRY A FRIEND,
I TAKE THAT AS A SIGN.
WE'LL HAVE SEVEN BABIES,
AND A BED WITH LINENS FINE.
OH ANDRÉ DON'T YOU WAIT.
COME AND KISS ME BY THE GATE.
MY MOM HAS SET THE DATE!
WE'LL LIVE BY THE SHORE OF THE PORCUPINE RIVER,
IN A HOUSE THAT'S VERY REFINED.

> André is now faced with three "Minnies." All of his buddies still sport their handkerchiefs on their heads. They surround André pulling him this direction and that as though fighting over him.

ANDRÉ
I HAVE TO BE BLUNT FAIR MINNIE
YOU'VE GOT TO LET GO OF ME!

> They let go of him.

J.R., WILL AND JOHN GUALEY
OH, I AGREE!

JOHN GUALEY
YOU'VE GOT TO GET DRESSED!

         WILL
WE'RE MEETING THE PRIEST!

       J.R.,WILL AND JOHN GUALEY
I'VE MADE AN APPOINTMENT AT NINE!

         J.R.
MY MOM MADE THE CAKE.

         WILL
THERE'S PLENTY OF TIME.

       J.R.,WILL AND JOHN GUALEY
REMEMBER YOUR HEART IS MINE!

> The men drop their high pitch voices down to regular sound.

      J.R.,WILL AND JOHN GUALEY (cont'd)
YOU'LL LIVE BY THE SHORE OF THE PORCUPINE RIVER.

         ANDRÉ
I AM DOOMED BY THE SHORE OF THE PORCUPINE RIVER!

       J.R.,WILL AND JOHN GUALEY
IN A HOUSE THAT'S VERY...
IN A HOUSE THAT'S VERY
REFINED.

> The guys laugh together, their handkerchiefs still on their heads.

7   **EXT. PORCUPINE CAMP MAIN STREET - MINNIE HAS SOME LAUNDRY TO DO**

> Minnie, a young pretty girl, who also looks very tough, enters. She is wielding her mom's rug beater. J.R., Will and John Gualey quickly take the handkerchiefs off their heads. Will and John hide André behind them.
>
> Maggie, a middle aged Chippewa guide, also enters. She holds her head high, (she was called "Princess" and respected by many.) She sets out a sign, guide services and stands to wait for the train, watching Minnie and André with wry interest.

MINNIE
You boys seen André?

J.R.
Not in a while.

MINNIE
Really. Who's that back there?

J.R.
In a short while.

ANDRÉ
Cheri!

MINNIE
Don't cheri me, André LeRoux. I know I'm not your cheri.

ANDRÉ
I was just looking for you.

MINNIE
Mmhmm, under a wagon?

ANDRÉ
You're so pretty today Minnie. Is that a new um, outfit you're wearing?

MINNIE
No. It isn't.

> J.R. snickers and Will elbows André. Nodding towards Minnie, John Gualey indicates his hair.

ANDRÉ
Quels beaux cheveux, Minnie... Comme la crinière d'un cheval.

> Will gives him a meaningful look but Minnie is smitten by the words.

André (cont'd)
Un cheval qui se lave... et... se brosse...

MINNIE
Oh, when you say things in french you make me forget everything. Don't make me angrier than I am, André LeRoux.

J.R.
I think I'd listen to her André.

MINNIE
You led me on André.

ANDRÉ
I never told you anything but the truth. We're friends, we have a lot in common...

> Minnie starts tapping her rug beater against her leg. The train has obviously stopped and new people are entering. All the locals though are watching Minnie and André.

MINNIE
Oh, your words, your fine, fine words. What was it you said last night? And don't you dare say it in french! You know what that does to me.

ANDRÉ
I just said that we have similar interests.

MINNIE
Uh, huh. Similar interests. Did you hear that boys?

JOHN GUALEY
Uh huh.

WILL
Oh yeah.

J.R.
Anything you say Minnie.

ANDRÉ
Why are you mad at me? I didn't say we should get married!

MINNIE
Why you! You have some nerve, to lead a girl on; we've been dating for six months now.

ANDRÉ
Dating? Dating?! Minnie, I just thought you were interested in trains!

MINNIE
Why did I hang my hat for you? Last night I gave you every opportunity to ask me to marry you. We went to our favorite tree, and sat in the moonlight; I wore my favorite dress; I even put a flower in my hair!

> Just out of sight of Minnie, J.R. pretends to be Minnie wearing a hat. John Gualey and Will snicker, but elbow him to be quiet.

MINNIE (cont'd)
It was perfect, André, the perfect night for a proposal. And now I see you've just made me a fool. A right fine fool André LeRoux. A fool for believing you at all. And there I was, all ready for saying I do.

> J.R., Will and John Gualey snicker to themselves.

MINNIE (cont'd)
What is it? What's so funny? Is there someone else?

> J.R., Will and John Gualey look at each other with wide eyes.

MINNIE (cont'd)
Well, I won't be made a laughing stock anymore. If you don't love me André, then who do you love? Who is it? Or do I have to beat it out of you?

ANDRÉ
No, there's no one Minnie. I just want to be free, that's all.

> Minnie becomes dangerously quiet, tapping her rug beater against her hand. Will elbows André and looks at him meaningfully.

WILL
Go on, André, tell her about your fiancée.

ANDRÉ
Quoi?

MINNIE
Fiancée?

                        J.R.
It will be easier if you just tell her.

                        JOHN GUALEY
Might be, otherwise you'll be hearing from her mother too. She
knocked out a wrestler...

                        ANDRÉ
Oh, oh yes. Well, my fiancée...

                        MINNIE
Is that why you wouldn't get engaged? Why you! Who is she? I'd
like to meet her. Who is it?

                                   She starts to back him up towards the train.

                        MINNIE (cont'd)
Who is it André?

                                   Caroline, a dreamy young lady wearing a long
                                   pretty dress and small pistols on each hip, walks
                                   off the train into the town. She walks over to
                                   where her bags are, which is near Minnie and
                                   André. She is absorbed in a book and doesn't see
                                   what is going on. André notices her though. He
                                   grabs her.

                        ANDRÉ
Mon Coeur! I'm glad you made it.

                                   André spins Caroline around, dips her in his arms
                                   and plants a big kiss. Caroline is so surprised she
                                   doesn't react at first. Minnie looks shocked.

                        MINNIE
You are such a liar, André. You can't have everything you know;
someday it will catch up with you. You may think you like freedom,
and *trains*, but someday you'll wish you could get married and stay
put.

                                   Minnie turns to Caroline.

                        MINNIE (cont'd)
I hope you break his heart. He will never stick by you, Mr.Adventure.

> Minnie stomps off. André laughs, but as he turns once more to Caroline he discovers that he is looking down the barrel of her gun.

8   **EXT. PORCUPINE CAMP - CAROLINE HATES ANDRÉ**

CAROLINE
Hello. Kindly unhand me, sir. I'm not sure what treatment you are used to here in the North but where I come from a woman knows how to handle herself.

> André slowly releases her.

JOHN GUALEY
Oh, you'll fit right in, miss.

> J.R. snickers. Caroline points her gun at him as well.

CAROLINE
Anyone else?

J.R.
No, no. I wasn't laughing at you ma'am.

CAROLINE
Very well. Can one of you *gentlemen* point me in the direction of the supply office and a good guide?

ANDRÉ
Tu parles! You're a prospector?

CAROLINE
Of course I am. Why, you don't think a woman can find gold?

JOHN GUALEY
He didn't say that. You just look so... dressed up.

CAROLINE
Men.

WILL
Do you have any idea what the bush is like up here?

JR.
No, she arrived by train.

CAROLINE
Of course, I'm well prepared.

> André picks up her book.

ANDRÉ
What, with this? What's the title, "Gold Rush Prospecting?" You'd be better off with Women's Quarterly.

CAROLINE
I'll have you know sir, that I have a lot of experience handling dangerous creatures. I have been in the wilderness before and let me tell you it is nothing compared to the streets of New York.

J.R.
I don't know about that, lady. I'm willing to bet this is the first time you've seen this many trees.

JOHN GUALEY
You had better get right back on that train. You'll die in a day out here, guide or no guide.

CAROLINE
I'm not leaving. I have as much right to be here as you.

ANDRÉ
Have you ever met a bear? The claws will make pâté out of you.

CAROLINE
I can take care of myself, thank you very much.

ANDRÉ
Mon Dieu, tu est folle. Are you going to wave your little pistol at it? That should work.

CAROLINE
My gun is not for bears.

> John Gualey whistles low.

JOHN GUALEY
You sure know how to pick 'em André.

> Song starts....

ANDRÉ
You should get right back on that train, it is way too dangerous out here for sight seeing. Bonne chance. This one pulls out, the next one isn't due for a few days.

CAROLINE
I'm not going. Who are you anyway? Why do you care if I'm here or not?

9 **EXT. PORCUPINE CAMP - CAROLINE AND ANDRÉ AGREE TO DISAGREE**

CAROLINE
IT'S JUST LIKE A MAN
TO ACT LIKE A KING,
AND ORDER A WOMAN AROUND.
IT'S JUST LIKE A MAN,
HE'LL DO AS HE PLEASES,
LEAVE WOMEN THE MESS THAT HE'S FOUND.
IT'S JUST LIKE A MAN,
TO THINK THAT A WOMAN
CAN'T HANDLE HERSELF ON HER OWN!
BUT MEN ARE JUST BOYS,
QUAKING AND SHAKING,
FRIGHTENED OF BEING ALONE.

ANDRÉ
IT'S LIKE A WOMAN
TO THINK SHE COMMANDS
EVERY MAN AND THE WORLD'S DAILY TURN.
IT'S LIKE A WOMAN
TO LOOK AT A MAN,
IMAGINE WHAT'S BEST JUST FOR HER!
YOU BET A WOMAN
WILL DO ANYTHING,
THEY'LL TRICK YOU AND STICK YOU THE BLAME!
BUT GIRLS ARE JUST BABES,
WILD AND COMPLAINING,
HOPING FOR SOMEONE TO TAME!

> André pulls Caroline towards the train station as he does they begin to waltz, all the while Caroline tries to break free.

ANDRÉ (cont'd)
GO ON HOME, GO ON HOME LITTLE GIRL.
THE PORCUPINE CAMP IS NO PLACE FOR YOU.
GO ON HOME, GO ON HOME LITTLE GIRL.
THIS ISN'T A TAME AND CITYFIED ZOO.
IT'S NO PLACE TO STAY,
YOU'LL DIE IN A DAY...
AND I ALWAYS HATE FUNERALS, TOO.

The guys encourage André as he spins her in a waltz. Caroline breaks away from André's grip.

CAROLINE
GO ON HOME, GO ON HOME LITTLE BOY.
THE PORCUPINE CAMP IS NO PLACE FOR YOU.
GO ON HOME, GO ON HOME LITTLE BOY.
GO ON, LET YOUR MOTHER LOOK AFTER YOU.

NOW RUN ALONG HOME.

ANDRÉ
NO, YOU GO ON HOME.

CAROLINE
YOU FIRST!

ANDRÉ
YOU'RE ALONE.

CAROLINE
I'VE GOT GUNS, NOW GET OUT OF MY WAY!
BEING A WOMAN, I CAME HERE FOR GOLD,
AND BEING A WOMAN, I'LL STAY!

CAROLINE (cont'd)
I'll bet you that I'll find gold and I'll find it before you do. How long have you been here?

J.R.
Oh, he's been here ten months.

CAROLINE
Right then, what is the going bet? Let's say a dollar per month. Ten dollars?

John Gauley whistles low.

JOHN GUALEY
Ten Dollars. You sure know how to pick 'em.

WILL
Careful André, you don't have ten dollars.

ANDRÉ
I've got one better for you. If you find gold first, I'll leave.

CAROLINE
Sounds good to me.

ANDRÉ
But if I find it first, you leave...

CAROLINE
Fine.

ANDRÉ
... but not before telling Minnie all about our wedding plans.

CAROLINE
Fine.

ANDRÉ
Fine.

Caroline and André shake hands.

CAROLINE
It's a deal then. I'll find gold before you. I hope you're used to losing.

ANDRÉ
And I hope you've bought your train ticket!

The men start to walk off. Caroline collects her bags. Will takes André aside.

WILL
You're a fool, you know that? What are you going to do if you lose?

ANDRÉ
Pourquoi? Your map is a sure thing right?

WILL
Well, there's nothing for it but to just try. Listen, Christie is bringing in my gear, I'm meeting her at the drug store in one hour. Things like this won't stay quiet for long.

> Will and André begin to walk off. Will stops.

WILL (cont'd)
Promise me, you'll lay off the women until the gold is found and a deal is signed. Your word on that, or the deal's off.

ANDRÉ
My word. Pas de problème!

WILL
Good, because your taste in women is really bad my friend, really bad.

10 EXT. PORCUPINE CAMP - CAROLINE MEETS THE LOCAL GANG

> Caroline is having trouble with her bags. She pulls them along, kicking them in frustration because they are very heavy. Maggie watches her with interest. John Campsall and his friends, Rudi Puera and Gertrude Haas (a tom boy they call "Gert",) looking for a way to make money, approach Caroline to see if they can help her with her bags.

JOHN
Hey lady, do ya want a hand with that?

CAROLINE
I can handle this myself, thank you very much. It's not like you men don't have better things to do...

> Caroline looks up and notices that it is just a group of kids.

CAROLINE (cont'd)
Oh, I'm sorry. I'm not usually rude. It's just those men... they are so infuriating.

GERTRUDE
That's what my mom says. You've no need to be afraid of us lady, we just want to help.

JOHN
It's not like we're going to kiss you.

CAROLINE
Oh no? Well, that's a relief.

RUDI
I'm never going to kiss a girl ... yuck.

GERTRUDE
As though a girl would ever want to kiss you.

RUDI
Yuck. Double yuck.

CAROLINE
(Laughs) I feel better already children. You'll have to excuse me, I've been very rude.

She offers her hand.

CAROLINE (cont'd)
Miss Flowers, of New York city, and you are?

Gertrude cleans her hands on her pants and shakes Caroline's hand.

GERTRUDE
Gert Haas.

RUDI
She's not a boy Miss Flowers. Her name is Gertrude.

Gertrude
I can punch better than any boy and you know it.

CAROLINE
You don't have to punch him to prove it, Gert.

RUDI
Yeah, Gert.

> Rudi clicks his heels together, bows to Caroline and kisses her hand.

RUDI (cont'd)
Rudolf Alexander Puera the third.

> Gertrude wacks him on the shoulder and whispers in his ear.

GERTRUDE
What do you think you're doing? No kissing.

RUDI
My mom said this is how you do it. She made me practice.

GERTRUDE
Well, your mom is dumb.

RUDI
She is not. We come from royalty.

GERTRUDE
Oh yeah? Then how come you're here?

CAROLINE
It's fine, just fine. You did it perfectly Rudolf.

> Rudi elbows Gertrude.

RUDI
See?

> John steps forward.

JOHN
I'm John Campsall. I'm not going to be a gentleman. I'm going to be a cart driver, like Mr. Gualey.

CAROLINE
That's an honorable job, John.

> John makes a little bow to her.

JOHN
You look like you could use help with your bags. We're very strong.

CAROLINE
I'm sure you are. Well, I could use a little help and you do look like nice children.

RUDI
We are nice children.

> Gertrude elbows Rudi. Caroline gets her little purse out to pay them.

CAROLINE
Listen, I need to find a good guide and a place to stay. Do you know anyone who can take me through the bush?

RUDI
If you want my advice Miss Flowers, you'll want the best guide there is. You'll want Maggie Buffalo.

JOHN
That's right. She can track a rabbit to its hole and her trap lines are never empty. If anyone could find you gold, it would be her.

GERTRUDE
It wouldn't be too bad for you. You're not a kid. She's always pinching my cheeks.

RUDI
And looking at you with those sad, sad eyes.

JOHN
And she sees everything. She always tells my mom where I am.

CAROLINE
I'll try to keep that in mind.

GERTRUDE
My mom says that's because she lost her family, four little kids and her husband up by Kamascotia.

JOHN
That's terrible.

RUDI
She couldn't save them? She can't be that good of a hunter.

GERTRUDE
My mom says they got sick and died one by one. Their graves are still out there, on an island.

RUDI
That's creepy.

11   EXT. PORCUPINE CAMP - CAROLINE MEETS MAGGIE

> Caroline looks thoughtful.

CAROLINE
You say she's the best?

JOHN
She's the best. Come on, we'll take you to her. Your stuff will be ok here. She's right by the drug store.

> John leads Caroline over to Maggie.

JOHN (cont'd)
Miss Flowers, this is Maggie Buffalo.

> Caroline stretches her hand out. Maggie takes it, looking her over cautiously.

CAROLINE
I'm very pleased to meet you. I am a prospector in need of a guide.

> Maggie's eyes open wider, she looks at Caroline with interest.

MAGGIE
Are you now?

CAROLINE
I have it on good report that you are the best guide there is and I am wondering if your services would be available. I am prepared to pay good money.

MAGGIE
I might be available.

> Maggie turns to John and children.

MAGGIE (cont'd)
John Campsall, your mother has been looking for you again.

> The children groan and John looks around.

MAGGIE (cont'd)
She's not here. But you should go home. It is not good to worry your mother. Maybe she will break her heart. A mother is no mother with a broken heart.

JOHN
Nah. Not my mom, she'd be glad if she didn't have to look after me.

MAGGIE
You had better go home John Campsall.

> John reluctantly skulks off, but it is obvious he doesn't intend to go home. Maggie turns her attention to Rudi and Gertrude.

MAGGIE (cont'd)
Look, you children take Miss Flowers' bags to the hotel for her, I'm sure she'll tip you.

CAROLINE
Well, I...

MAGGIE
If you pay them a good tip they'll sweep the mattress for you.

> The children take her bags to the hotel.

CAROLINE
Why would they do that?

MAGGIE
Bed bugs.

CAROLINE
Oh. Alright then. Make sure it's extra clean children!

MAGGIE
So, Miss Flowers, I see you've met André LeRoux.

CAROLINE
(Sighs) Oh, I thought men here would be different. Less... infuriating.

> Maggie smiles.

MAGGIE
You don't need to meet many men to know the whole animal. Men were made to make women crazy. You are a strange lady. How badly do you want to win your bet?

CAROLINE
You have no idea. I want to win, it would put him in his place. And I need the money, the sooner, the better.

> Maggie grabs Caroline's arm and turns it over, looking at the muscles. She takes off Caroline's glove.

CAROLINE (cont'd)
What are you doing?

MAGGIE
At least you're tougher than you look. Are you as strong in the legs?

CAROLINE
I'm very strong, thank you very much.

MAGGIE
You can't be collapsing on me. I have enough to carry, and I'm not carrying you or your things.

CAROLINE
You won't have to. I can take care of myself.

MAGGIE
We'll see. Your fingers are very strong, but no callouses. What is it you do?

CAROLINE
I play piano.

MAGGIE
Play piano? You were lying about being in the wilderness before weren't you?

> Caroline sighs.

CAROLINE
There was a bush lot near my family's farm.

Maggie looks Caroline up and down.

MAGGIE
You'll have to do. I have an offer for you. There is a piece of land, it's far into the bush. The thing is, Will Bannerman, André's friend, he knows about it too. Some people think that I don't know much, but I see things, and the things I seen lately are worth looking at. There's gold there, I'm certain of it. It hasn't been staked yet, but we have to go today. Right away.

CAROLINE
Oh, I haven't even got my trunk settled yet, I...

MAGGIE
Do you want to win this bet or not?

CAROLINE
Yes, I... Yes.

MAGGIE
Good. The deal is, I'll take you there, but any find we make is split, even and fair. I think I can trust you; can I trust you?

Maggie looks Caroline clear in the eye. Caroline returns her gaze.

CAROLINE
You can trust me, as you can see, I'm not a good liar.

MAGGIE
Good.

CAROLINE
Why don't you just go there on your own?

Maggie looks at Caroline.

MAGGIE
Were you born under a bush? No permit, no claim. No people, no treaty, no home. I am an Indian, I'm not allowed to hold a claim for the land I was born on. My husband and children are all buried under the ground. I live nowhere, no place.

CAROLINE
That doesn't seem right. Do you really have no one?

12 **EXT. PORCUPINE CAMP/MEMORY WORLD -THE RIVER KNOWS - SONG**

> Maggie pauses for a moment. She remembers... The drum beat sounds as various people from the Porcupine Camp enter; Miners, Prospectors, Shop Keepers, School Teachers etc., and four small Chippewa children walk slowly in a line toward the stage to the beat of the drum. Maggie and Caroline do not notice the people for they are "Maggie's Memories," an embodiment of all the people she has met in her life. Maggie's Memories begin to sing in Maggie's native language (Ojibwe) The words "Zeebeh Gee Kendahn" translate as "The River Knows."

MAGGIE'S MEMORIES
ZEE-BEH GEE KEN-DAHN, ZEE-BEH GEE KEN-DAHN...

> Maggie stands surrounded by her memories, yet alone in the center of the stage.

MAGGIE
THE RIVER KNOWS
SHE CAN FIND HER WAY ALONE,
BROKEN TREES OR GRANITE STONE
WON'T DISMAY HER.

THE RIVER KNOWS
THAT A PATH IS NOT A HOME,
SHE IS HAPPIER TO ROAM
ANYWHERE NOW.

THE RIVER GOES
ALWAYS WILD AND RUNNING FREE,
NEVER WONDERING WHERE TO TURN
WHEN OR WHY.

THE RIVER'S WISE
MOVING ON NOT LOOKING BACK,
KEEPING NOTHING THOUGH SHE LACK
SHE DON'T MIND.

BUT I AM ALONE.
AND I AM NOT THE RIVER.
HOW TO FIND MY WAY,
WHEN I CAN'T FIND ME?

Caroline joins Maggie at center stage.

CAROLINE
TO BE ALONE,
YOU MUST TAKE HOLD OF YOURSELF,
PUT TOMORROW ON THE SHELF,
AND GO ON.

I'VE BEEN ALONE,
IN A ROOM SO FULL OF FRIENDS
THAT THE PITY NEVER ENDS
IN THEIR EYES.

MAGGIE, CAROLINE
WHEN YOU'RE ALONE,
THERE'S NO CHOICE BUT TO GO ON,
HOPING YOU WILL STAND UP STRONG
LIFE GOES BY.

BUT YOU'RE ALONE
AND THE CHOICES THAT YOU MAKE
ARE JUST YOURS AND YOURS TO TAKE
FAIL OR RISE.

MAGGIE
THE MORE I TURN, AND TRY, I COME TO FIND,

CAROLINE
I TURN, I TRY, I COME TO FIND,

CAROLINE AND MAGGIE
I CAN'T ACT ALONE.
FOR I WILL BE SWEPT FAR AWAY.
THEN NO-ONE WILL SEE ME PASS
OR THINK ON ME.

> Maggie's Memories, who have been watching and listening to everything Maggie has been singing, send the "Memories of Maggie's Children" to her. As the four children play near Maggie she looks up as though she hears something, but even though the children pass in front of her she still can not see them. "Maggie's Memories" sing "You are surrounded by love," in both Ojibwe and English.

MAGGIE'S MEMORIES
GA-WENISHE-KAY GAH-ZEE, YOU ARE SURROUNDED BY LOVE.
TZA GEE GO-WAH, TZA GEE GO-WAH.

> The "Memories of Maggie's Children," begin to circle Maggie and Caroline, walking slowly around the two women, finally coming to rest beside them. They lay reassuring hands on their shoulders. Caroline and Maggie finally look at each other with understanding.

MAGGIE
IF YOU AND I ACT TOGETHER,

> The "Memories of Maggie's Children" raise their hands encouragingly and Maggie and Caroline shake hands in agreement.

MAGGIE, CAROLINE
WE CAN MAKE A RIVER.
THEN NOTHING WILL BAR OUR WAY
FROM MOVING ON.

MAGGIE'S MEMORIES
ZEE-BEH GEE KEN-DAHN, ZEE-BEH GEE KEN-DAHN. TZA GEE GOH.

> The "Memories of Maggie's Children walk away from Caroline and Maggie to join the other memories. Maggie and Caroline look around, still touched by the magic in the air.

CAROLINE
We'll work together Maggie, just you and me.

>   Maggie and Caroline shake hands, Maggie looking
>   Caroline once more in the eye.

MAGGIE
Good, it's settled. I'll meet you at the drug store in one hour for supplies. You can't tell anyone that I know where the gold is, do you understand? Very important.

CAROLINE
I understand.

MAGGIE
And get better shoes, this isn't the city. Do you have money? Staking permit? Good. Oh and Caroline.

CAROLINE
Yes?

MAGGIE
If you see John Campsall, send him home to his mother. It is not good to miss your child.

>   Maggie and Caroline exit. Everyone is off the stage
>   except for Pearl.

13 EXT. PORCUPINE CAMP - PEARL AND JOHN PLAN TO FIND GOLD

>   Pearl is drawing with a stick in the dirt, singing.
>
>   John comes up behind her and hits her with a small
>   rock from a slingshot. She sits up.

PEARL
Hey! John! John Campsall! What did you do that for?

>   John shrugs.

JOHN
What ya doing Pearl Crawford O'Day? You been sitting there all morning.

PEARL
None of your business. It hurts.

JOHN
Come on, Pearl. It was just a little stone. Quit complaining.

PEARL
I'm not talking to you.

> John mimics her.

JOHN
I'm not talking to you.

PEARL
I'm not talking to you, stop it.

JOHN
I'm not talking to you, stop it.

> They start talking at the same time.

PEARL AND JOHN
I'm not talking to you, not talking to you, no, not talking, not talkiiiiiiing!

> Pearl coughs a lot.

JOHN
I win.

PEARL
You did not! I swallowed a fly. That doesn't count.

JOHN
So what are you doing?

PEARL
None of your business. I wouldn't tell you even if I wanted to.

JOHN
So you want to?

PEARL
Arrgh. Have ye any sense at all? You're no better than Mr.LeRoux.

JOHN
Well, you might as well tell me, I did see you anyway. You were staring at the ground, really hard.

> Pearl hesitates, then sighs.

> PEARL
> I was coming up with a plan, you see.

> JOHN
> Really? Well, let's have it.

>> Pastor Ad Schwidder walks into town from the bush, carrying a sack on his back. He watches the kids curiously as he leans against the hotel.

> PEARL
> I've been thinking. There's lots of gold out here...

> JOHN
> Everyone seems to find some.

> PEARL
> Not everyone. But I have a plan. I've been readn' that with the right composition of quartz and the lay of the land you can be sure of gold. Finding it, with tools and a partner, we could make lots of money. Be the first kids to find gold.

> JOHN
> That sounds good. Need a partner?

> PEARL
> Sure. Every team needs more than one person. I was just trying to figure who would go with me. It will be dangerous you know.

14 **EXT. PORCUPINE CAMP - PASTOR SCHWIDDER GETS IN ON THE PLAN**

>> Pastor Schwidder steps forward, a glint in his eye.

> PASTOR SCHWIDDER
> Why, Miss O'Day and Little John! What kind of plan are you making today? You're not going to build a boat are you?

> JOHN
> No sir, Pastor Schwidder.

> PASTOR SCHWIDDER
> That is a relief. I'd rather not fish you out of Porcupine Lake again... Or listen to your mother scream. I think I was deaf for a week.

> JOHN
> You should hear her at home.

PASTOR SCHWIDDER
Just don't give her too much to scream *about* John, that's all I ask. Now, what are these plans? Perhaps I can help before you get into trouble.

PEARL
I've a good plan, but you can't be telling anyone. We be looking for gold.

PASTOR SCHWIDDER
Oh, for gold. Of course. This is the place for it. But you won't be going down any mine shafts, will you?

> John elbows Pearl to keep her quiet.

JOHN
Nah! It should be easy to find. Everyone says the streets are paved with gold.

PASTOR SCHWIDDER
Yes, I've heard that.

> He leans in towards them as though whispering a secret, a twinkle in his eye.

PASTOR SCHWIDDER (cont'd)
I wonder why it looks so much like wood then? Very deceiving!

> Pastor Schwidder pretends to pry up one of the boards on the boardwalk.

PASTOR SCHWIDDER (cont'd)
Why look, it's just like Heaven!

> Pastor Schwidder sings.

PASTOR SCHWIDDER (cont'd)
JERUSALEM THE GOLDEN, WITH MILK AND HONEY BLEST!
THE PROMISE OF SALVATION, THE HOPE OF PEACE AND REST...

> The kids laugh as they try to stop him.

PEARL

It's not actually gold! We be looking in the woods. I've been reading all about gold. Mrs.Bannerman lends me any book I like from her house and the last one was prospecting.

PASTOR SCHWIDDER

In the woods? Pearl, your mother hasn't been well. Running off into the woods wouldn't be a good idea. You wouldn't want to make her worry.

PEARL

Well...

    John elbows Pearl.

JOHN

We're only playing, Pastor Schwidder.

PASTOR SCHWIDDER

Is that right Pearl?

    Pearl nods. Pastor Schwidder regards them cautiously.

PASTOR SCHWIDDER (cont'd)

Alright then.

JOHN

See...

PEARL AND JOHN

15 **EXT. PORCUPINE CAMP - COME ON, COME ON - SONG**

PEARL AND JOHN
COME ON, COME ON, TO THE PORCUPINE,
WHERE THE STREETS ARE MADE OF GOLD!
PICK UP YOUR THINGS,
LEAVE YOUR CARES BEHIND,
BY TONIGHT WE'LL HAVE WEALTH UNTOLD.
FOR I'M A ONE,
YOU'RE A ONE,
ONE AND ONE MAKE TWO,
GOLD WILL MAKE OUR WORRIES FALL THROUGH.
COME ON, COME ON, WE'VE GOT GOLD TO FIND,
BID OUR WORRIES AND CARES ADIEU.

                  PEARL
WHAT'CHA GONNA BUY, WHAT'CHA GONNA BUY JOHN?

                  JOHN
COAL BLACK MARE AND A STABLE TOO.
WHAT'CHA GONNA BUY, WHAT'CHA GONNA BUY PEARL?

                  PEARL
A BALL GOWN WITH LACE ECRU.

                  JOHN
   Eww.

                  Pearl sticks her tongue out at him.

                  PEARL AND JOHN
COME ON, COME ON, WE'VE GOT GOLD TO FIND,
BID OUR WORRIES AND CARES ADIEU.

                  Other children and adults join in as they walk to
                  the stores or the train, dancing and singing until the
                  stage is full of life.

                  PEARL AND JOHN, PASTOR SCHWIDDER
                  AND CHORUS
COME ON, COME ON TO THE PORCUPINE,
WHERE THE STREETS ARE MADE OF GOLD!
PICK UP YOUR THINGS,
LEAVE YOUR CARES BEHIND,
BY TONIGHT WE'LL HAVE WEALTH UNTOLD.
FOR I'M A ONE,
YOU'RE A ONE,
ONE AND ONE MAKE TWO,
GOLD WILL MAKE OUR WORRIES FALL THROUGH.
COME ON, COME ON, WE'VE GOT GOLD TO FIND,
BID OUR WORRIES AND CARES ADIEU.

                  PEARL
WHAT'CHA GONNA BUY, WHAT'CHA GONNA BUY PASTOR?

                  PASTOR SCHWIDDER
NEW SNOWSHOES AND A BOOT OR TWO.

                  JOHN
WHAT'CHA GONNA BUY, WHAT'CHA GONNA BUY PASTOR?

       PASTOR SCHWIDDER
A NEW BOAT FOR EACH OF YOU.

       PASTOR SCHWIDDER (cont'd)
 Just don't drown.

      PEARL AND JOHN AND PASTOR
       SCHWIDDER AND CHORUS
COME ON, COME ON TO THE PORCUPINE,
WHERE THE STREETS ARE MADE OF GOLD!
PICK UP YOUR THINGS,
LEAVE YOUR CARES BEHIND,
BY TONIGHT WE'LL HAVE WEALTH UNTOLD.
FOR I'M A ONE,
YOU'RE A ONE,
ONE AND ONE MAKE TWO,
GOLD WILL MAKE OUR WORRIES FALL THROUGH.
COME ON, COME ON, WE'VE GOT WEALTH TO FIND,
BID OUR WORRIES AND CARES ADIEU.

COME ON, COME ON, WE'VE GOT WEALTH TO FIND,
BID OUR WORRIES AND CARES ADIEU.

          The crowd goes off into the various businesses etc.
          Leaving Pearl, John and Pastor Schwidder near
          centre stage.

       PASTOR SCHWIDDER
 You two stay out of trouble, fine?

        JOHN
 Fine! You can trust us, Pastor Schwidder.

          Pastor Schwidder turns and smiles at them.

       PASTOR SCHWIDDER
 Not too much trouble, alright kinder?

          Pastor Schwidder picks up his pack and starts to
          walk off past the hotel. John turns and speaks
          quietly to Pearl.

16 EXT. PORCUPINE CAMP - THE LADIES OF THE PORCUPINE ROUND UP THE TROUBLEMAKERS

> Mrs.Campsall, a cross-looking, overworked woman and Jeanna Weiss, a middle-aged Finnish woman arrive they are both carrying a baby. Christy Bannerman, young and pleasant with a mischievous smile, is with them. Pastor Schwidder stops and greets them loudly, positioning himself so that they are no longer looking in the direction of the children.

PASTOR SCHWIDDER
Good morning ladies. Mrs.Campsall, Mrs.Weiss, Mrs.Bannerman.

> Pearl and John don't notice Pastor Schwidder's hint and continue talking.

JEANNA
Good morning Pastor Schwidder, are you come from Wabewawa?

PASTOR SCHWIDDER
Yes, I started last week through the bush. It is so hot and dry, the mud up by Fredrick House is nearly a beach. Makes for easy going, yes?

JEANNA
To be sure. Have you been seeing my Robert?

PASTOR SCHWIDDER
No, I haven't Jeanna. But I only just arrived. Did you try the mine?

JEANNA
Not yet heir Pastor Schwidder, but the men came looking for him at the house this morning. So! He is not there. Good morning to you.

PASTOR SCHWIDDER
Good morning to you all, ladies. I must be off to set my camp.

> Pastor Schwidder exits shaking his head at Pearl and John who are still so busy making plans that they do not see John's mother. Mrs.Campsall sees them though. She is not impressed

JOHN
So when do we start?

> PEARL

This evening at the big campfire. We'll be back before they even know we're gone!

> *They shake hands.*

> JOHN

Meet at the end of the street, first line of trees in the bush? Deal?

> PEARL

Deal.

> *Mrs.Campsall raises her voice.*

> MRS.CAMPSALL

John Campsall! What do you think you're doing? You are supposed to be home right now helping your sister with the wood.

> JOHN

Awh, mom! I was going to.

> MRS.CAMPSALL

Never you mind going to, John. Don't be all sneaky eyed with me. When I ask you to do something I expect you to do it!

> JOHN

Just a sec. I'm not quite done.

> MRS.CAMPSALL

Oh ho! You had better believe me you're done young man. Done like dinner. That wood is heavy and I asked you both to get at it. You can't expect your sister to do all that work herself, and the wood isn't about to chop itself.

> JOHN

Alright.

> MRS.CAMPSALL

Now, John. Now! Get moving.

> *John makes like he is moving on but then ducks back around the building when his mother is not looking.*

MRS.CAMPSALL (cont'd)
I swear, that boy will be the death of me. You can see it in his eyes, I don't know what he's up to but it's something.

CHRISTY
I'm sure it's nothing to worry about.

MRS.CAMPSALL
Oh. I can tell. You'll tell too when you're a mother, Christy. A mother's intuition: just gives me the chills down the spine, right here.

CHRISTY
Now, if only you could harness that intuition for gold finding.

MRS.CAMPSALL
Ha! I'd be a rich woman there's no doubt about that!

> Mrs.Campsall catches John again, this time by the ear. She and John exit stage right, scolding him the whole time.

JEANNA
And where will we be Ariel? Your pa will be fired and who will feed us then?

CHRISTY
Don't you worry Jeanna, we'll find him soon.

JEANNA
And me with no sleep, all the up and down and Ariel crying and crying and still, now I chase him!

CHRISTY
It isn't that bad, you'll see.

JEANNA
You are first year married, you'll see.

> Mrs.O'Day exits the Drug store. Pearl helps her mother cross the street. Christy sees her.

CHRISTY
Mrs.O'Day! I beg your pardon, you didn't happen to see Mr.Weiss in there, did you?

MRS. O'DAY
Oh hello Jeanna, Christy. If you be looking for your husband, he's in there with the elephant if you ask me. And a ruckus for this time of day too. I'll be going home for a little more peace and quiet. To think they sell headache medicine in there!

JEANNA
With the elephant?

Christy mimes drinking.

JEANNA (cont'd)
Oh! No he's not! That man! That man!

17 **INT. DRUG STORE - ROBERT, FRANK AND THE DRUG STORE PARTY**

As Christy and Jeanna walk through the door the store "opens" up so that we can see inside. There are a few tables. A long drug store counter with the typical wall of small square drawers behind them. Lillian Knapp cooks madly behind one of the counters dishing out food to the locals. It is clear that the drug store also operates as a "blind pig." A number of the patrons seem to have imbibed a bit too much. It is lively and fun inside. The women are momentarily jostled around as they look for their loved ones.

Frank, responding to some comment makes fun of Robert.

FRANK
That's ridiculous! All hail, Robert Weiss, the only man in the Porcupine who isn't here for gold!

ROBERT WEISS
That's right boys!

Robert Weiss is the centre of attention.

ROBERT WEISS (cont'd)
IT'S TOO HOT FOR WORK'N
LET'S LIFT UP A GLASS.
DREAMING OF GOLD IT WILL
MAKE HOURS PASS.

I WISH YOU A HOME,
AND A LIFE YOU LIVE WELL.
FINE FRIENDS ON YOUR DOORSTEP
AND STORIES TO TELL.

FRANK
HERE'S TO AULD LANG SYNE
THE SWEETEST REFRAIN.
I'D TRADE ALL OF THIS
FOR A SPOT ON THE TRAIN.

CHORUS
THERE'D BE NO BED BUGS,
NO SEES,
HEAT STROKE,
I'D FINALLY FEEL RAIN,

I'D TRADE ALL OF THIS
FOR A SPOT ON THE TRAIN.

J.R.
IT'S TOUGH TO GET USED TO
BUT I'LL GUARANTEE,
THERE'S MAGIC AROUND US
IT STEALS SILENTLY.

YOU MAY GO ON HOME
TO LAND YOU KNOW WELL,
BUT YOUR HEART'S IN THE NORTHLAND
WHERE SILENT THOUGHTS DWELL.

FRANK
SAY WHAT YOU LIKE
I WON'T MISS IT A BIT!
I'D SELL ALL YOUR SILENCE
FOR A ROOM AT THE RITZ.

CHORUS
THERE'D BE NO BED BUGS,
NO WASPS,
FRUIT FLIES,
NO LICE, NO BEES,
GALL WASPS, BLACK FLIES, HOUSE FLIES, NO FLEAS.

I'D FINALLY FEEL RAIN!
I'D TRADE ALL OF THIS FOR A SPOT ON THE TRAIN.

                    FRANK
WHEN I FIND GOLD,
THE WORLD WILL BOW.
WHEN I FIND GOLD...
WHO CARES ABOUT HOW!
THEY'LL SPREAD THE NEWS,
I'M ABSOLUTELY, INCONTROVERTIBLY POWERFUL NOW!

I'D PACK ALL MY BAGS,
I'D FINALLY BE FREE.
I'D WEAR MYSELF OUT TAKING GOOD CARE OF ME!

                    CHORUS
THERE'D BE NO BED BUGS,
NO WASPS,
FRUIT FLIES,
NO LICE, NO BEES,
GALL WASPS, BLACK FLIES, HOUSE FLIES, NO FLEAS.

MOSQUITOS! MOSQUITOES! MOSQUITOES! MOSQUITOES!
THE ITCHING AND SCRATCHING AND THOUGHTS OF THEM HATCHING
WILL FINALLY DRIVE YOU INSANE!
I HOPE WE GET RAIN!
I'D TRADE ALL OF THIS FOR A SPOT ON THE TRAIN!

              ANDRÉ, FRANK, JR AND JOHN GUALEY
NO NEED TO CONVINCE ME
THE ANSWER IS PLAIN.

                    CHORUS
BOYS, SAVE ME A SPOT 'CAUSE IT'S ONLY HUMANE.

                      ALL
I'D TRADE ALL OF THIS FOR A SPOT ON THE TRAIN.

                    An angry Jeanna pulls Robert Weiss from the drug
                    store, as the men wave good-bye to him.

18   **INT. DRUG STORE - ANDRÉ GETS SOME ADVICE**

                    André comes up to the counter to order something
                    from Lillian.

> Frank Harson sits nearby nursing a drink but also listening surreptitiously. Will sees Christy and goes over to her.

ANDRÉ
Salut Lillian. Do you have what I asked for?

> Lillian looks him up and down with a sure eye.

LILLIAN
Ah, André my boy. Going into the bush are you? You boys better be careful. You've heard about the fires we've been having the last few days? The Dome nearly lost their site not two days ago. If it wasn't for the bucket brigade that would have been the end of it.

ANDRÉ
J'ai entendu dire! They have some good men up there.

LILLIAN
You best not take the bacon, you'll be needing a fire for that. And one spark, whoosh.

ANDRÉ
That is true. What else you have? Something gourmet?

> Lillian laughs.

LILLIAN
Gourmet! Nothing but the best for my boys, you know it. There's a pickled pork roll. I can cut you some of that.

ANDRÉ
Magnifique.

> Frank Harson looks up, interested. You can see his intelligence working.

FRANK (WHISPERING)
Where are you boys going in such heat? Gold?

ANDRÉ
Oh, no. Camping, you know.

FRANK

Well, I'm not saying you are, but if you were, and you needed help with any kind of something *special*, you're sitting next to the guy who is best able to give it to you. You've heard of George Carmack? His find started the Klondike rush... Well, it's not widely passed about but I taught him everything he knows.

ANDRÉ

Is that so? Thanks for the offer, but we're going camping.

Frank doesn't believe him.

LILLIAN

Now Frank, you're not bending my André's ear are you? Telling him tales?

FRANK

Of course not, Lillian. Right André?

ANDRÉ

Sure.

LILLIAN

Alright then Frank. Did you want a refill?

Frank shakes his head.

LILLIAN (cont'd)

I'll come back in a while, maybe then.

Frank turns back to nursing his mug of beer and Lillian turns to André.

19 **INT. DRUG STORE - LILLIAN EXPLAINS LOVE**

LILLIAN

Here's your pork André. I added a little jar of my special blueberry jelly. Now, don't go telling everyone. I wasn't able to make a lot of it. With all this heat I had to fend off the bears to get enough blueberries for one pot.

ANDRÉ

You are a good woman, Lillian. It's a pity more women aren't like you.

LILLIAN
Thank you André. Oh, you remind me so much of my Douglas. Especially when you smile like that. The women must love you.

ANDRÉ
Me? Fais moi pas rire! Did you not hear about Minnie?

LILLIAN
Oh, goodness, Minnie. Didn't you know what she was up to?

ANDRÉ
Quoi dire? Apparently I'm an idiot. No matter, I'm not looking for a wife at least until I become a conductor. And I need to find gold first before that will ever happen.

LILLIAN
Now, André, I wouldn't let one nosy, pushy, no good kind of girl drive you off.

ANDRÉ
I'm not going to worry about it. It's better to be alone anyway. Tout seul n'est-ce pas? It will make it easier to get where I need to go. The life of a train man is no life for a wife anyway. No women for me, no sir.

LILLIAN
Aren't you the clever one?

ANDRÉ
Quoi? I like to think so.

LILLIAN
You are like a ghost from the past, André LeRoux.

ANDRÉ
What is that supposed to mean?

LILLIAN
I've heard those words before. When you're young the world seems full of choices. Do you really think you can have it all, and when and where you like as well?

ANDRÉ
I don't know what you mean. Look at me Lillian, it is not as though I have the choice to love or not. I am alone n'est ce pas?
(MORE)

> ANDRé (cont'd)
> Perhaps alone is better. It is definitely easier. I'll just look out for me and what's best for me.

> LILLIAN
> You and I both know Minnie wasn't out to love you. If I were you, and I'm not, I know, I wouldn't let Minnie make my mind up. It is hard to go through life alone. You don't know it yet, André, but it's hard. The only reason Minnie tricked you was because you were so focused on far away, you missed where you are right now. If you open your eyes you never know what might happen.

20 **INT. DRUG STORE/MEMORY LAND - LILLIAN EXPLAINS LOVE - SONG**

> LILLIAN
> YOU'LL FIND LOVE'S
> NOT SOMETHING YOU CAN TAME,
> A SOFT AND GENTLE FLAME,
> IT PASSES AND IS LOST.
>
> WHEN YOU LOVE
> HOLD ON WITH ALL YOUR MIGHT,
> FOR LOVE ALONE IS WORTH YOUR LIFE.
>
> I ONCE LOVED
> WHEN TIME WAS JUST A GAME,
> AND LOVING WAS A NAME
> I SPOKE BUT NEVER KNEW.
>
> DON'T YOU WAIT
> FOR LOVE WILL PASS YOU BY
> AND WITH ITS LIGHT THE DARKNESS CRIES...

>> The chorus hums thoughtfully in the background as they go about their business in the drug store. Ladies eating lunch or buying supplies. Men nursing drinks or playing games etc.

> LILLIAN (cont'd)
> WHAT IS WORTH YOUR LOVE?
> IS THERE MORE YOU HAVE TO GAIN?
> LOVE IS LIKE THE SUN
> HE GIVES THE MOON HER FLAME.
> FOR LOVE MOVES THROUGH OUR LIVES SO QUICKLY
> NEVER PAUSING AT THE DOOR.

ALWAYS WATCH FOR LOVE
DO NOT WAIT ANYMORE.

                      ANDRÉ

THEY SAY LOVE
WILL MAKE YOUR SOUL TAKE FLIGHT,
BUT I'VE SEEN LOVERS FIGHT,
THEY BREAK THEIR VOWS AND MORE.

                      LILLIAN

TRUE, BUT LOVE
IS STRONGER THAN YOU GUESS,
LOVE CARRIES ON INSIDE DISTRESS.

> Chorus stops what they are doing and facing forward dreamily they sing.

                    LILLIAN (cont'd)

WHAT IS WORTH YOUR LOVE?
IS THERE MORE YOU HAVE TO GAIN?
FOR LOVE IS LIKE THE SUN,
HE GIVES THE MOON HER FLAME.

                      CHORUS

LOVE IS ALL.
FOR LOVE I'D GIVE ALL.

                LILLIAN AND ANDRÉ

OH WHAT IS WORTH MY LOVE?
IS THERE MORE YOU/I HAVE TO GAIN?
LOVE IS LIKE THE SUN
HE GIVES THE MOON HER FLAME.

                    CHORUS

OH LOVE IS MORE THAN ALL
I'D HOPE TO GAIN.

> The chorus dance with each other, memories of the ones they love but have left behind or lost.

            LILLIAN, ANDRÉ AND CHORUS

ALWAYS LOOK FOR LOVE (ANDRÉ AND CHORUS: LOVE)
DO NOT WAIT ANYMORE.

LILLIAN AND ANDRÉ
ALWAYS LOOK FOR LOVE (ANDRÉ: LOVE)
DO NOT WAIT ANYMORE.

> The lights go down on the bar as it "closes."

21 **INT. WEISS HOUSE - JEANNA AND ROBERT AND THE BUSH PARTY**

> On the other side of the stage Jeanna stands brushing her hair looking into a "mirror" while Robert Weiss rocks Ariel. Their "house" is represented by a few simple objects including a rocking chair, a cradle and a wash stand. Perhaps one of the walls/stores move to create one of the house walls.

JEANNA
Why were you there Robert? The men were looking for you this morning. What am I to say? You are not here, you are not there, you are giving the drink to everyone. You tell me.

ROBERT WEISS
I am telling you, it's fine Jeanna, I had to be in to meet the train, some Italians came off this morning.

JEANNA
You are impossible. You'll lose this place too and then what?

> Ariel begins to cry.

ROBERT WEISS
Shh, little Ariel, shh.

JEANNA
You're holding her wrong Robert. She likes to be walked, like a good Finnish baby.

> Jeanna demonstrates how to walk with a slight bounce. Robert bounces her on his belly.

ROBERT WEISS
Just like a ride on a German jelly roll, my little angel. Shh.

JEANNA
Not like that. She doesn't like it.

22 INT. WEISS HOUSE - LULLABY/WEISS LOVE SONG

> Robert sighs. Jeanna angrily turns back to brushing her hair while he rocks Ariel. As he sings the baby's crying begins to calm down until at last she is asleep.

ROBERT WEISS
YOU'RE SURE TO BE A LOVELY LADY,
THEY'LL ALL SAY WHAT A LOVELY LADY,
WITH EYES THAT SHINE SO BRIGHT,
SMILES OF SWEET DELIGHT,
BEST OF ALL IN SIGHT, THERE.

> Jeanna pauses to listen to Robert sing, gradually turning towards him.

ROBERT WEISS (cont'd)
WHY ARE YOU SUCH A LOVELY LADY?
HOW CAN YOU BE A LOVELY LADY?
YOUR MOTHER WHO YOU KNOW,
SETS THE WORLD AGLOW,
SHE'S GAVE YOU HER GLOW, FAIR.

> Jeanna smiles sadly.

JEANNA
I'm not able to do this Robert. Maybe I wasn't meant to be a mother. I can't stop her crying and I'm not sleeping, you're not sleeping, I burnt a whole roast... I just forgot... What is happening to me, Robert?

> Robert smiles at Jeanna and shakes his head. He sings to Ariel about Jeanna.

ROBERT WEISS
I'LL TELL YOU OF THIS LOVELY LADY,
YOU'LL HEAR ABOUT THIS LOVELY LADY,
FOR SHE'S LOVED HEART AND SOUL,
BY YOUR FATHER SO,
THAT IS WHY YOU'LL GROW, FAIR.

> Ariel stops crying, she is asleep. Robert gently lays her in her cradle then taking Jeanna by the waist, he spins her around.

                    ROBERT WEISS (cont'd)
EVERYONE HOPES TO FIND THEIR FUTURE
DIGGING DEEP IN HILLS OF GOLD.
THEY HOPE TO FIND THE ANSWER
IN WHAT IS BOUGHT AND SOLD.

I WISH EVERY MOMENT
BRINGS LIFE WITH YOU TO SHARE
I'D TRADE THOSE GOLDEN HILLSIDES
TO FIND YOU WAITING THERE.

TIME MAY CHANGE OUR LIVES COMPLETELY
CLOSING EVERY OPEN DOOR.
BRING ON EVERY CHANGING MOMENT

                ROBERT WEISS AND JEANNA
LOVE, I WOULD NOT ASK FOR MORE.

I WISH EVERY MOMENT
BRINGS LIFE WITH YOU TO SHARE
I'D TRADE THOSE GOLDEN HILLSIDES
TO FIND YOU WAITING THERE.

TIME MAY CHANGE OUR LIVES COMPLETELY
CLOSING EVERY OPEN DOOR.
BRING ON EVERY CHANGING MOMENT
LOVE, I WOULD NOT ASK FOR MORE.

> Robert Weiss and Jeanna embrace as the lights go down on their house.

23 **EXT. GOLDFIELD/FOREST - EVERYONE IS AFTER THE SAME GOLD**

> On the other side of the stage, Will says goodbye to Christy as André looks on.
>
> A crowd goes off to the party and Christy joins them, waving good-bye. Will watches her leave until she is out of sight. Finally, he picks up his gear.

                ANDRÉ
We'll be back in a few days, maybe sooner, who knows.

> Will turns back to André.

WILL
Sure. It's too bad we couldn't go to the party first, that's all.

ANDRÉ
Well, maybe one night makes no difference. We go to the party then stake our gold. Just a short walk in the bush and it is ours, n'est-ce pas? Nobody knows where but you.

> They pick up their stuff to go. Maggie and Caroline enter on the other side of the stage. Maggie is helping Caroline to get her stuff together. Will holds his hand up.

WILL
Shh.

ANDRÉ
Quoi?

WILL
Someone's here.

ANDRÉ
It could be anyone, it is a busy night. Big party, yes?

WILL
No, look.

> The music starts. André notices Caroline who still hasn't noticed them.

ANDRÉ
Pas elle! Why is she here?

WILL
We've got trouble André. Do you see who she's with?

ANDRÉ
Maggie Buffalo. Ce n'est pas bon. She's good, but we've got a sure thing, right?

                    WILL
I saw her out by our site the other day. André, she knows where our
gold is.

                    ANDRÉ
Well then, what are we waiting for? Allons-y!

                              Will and André run off. Maggie looks up.

                    MAGGIE
Did you see that?

                    CAROLINE
No.

                              Maggie looks at Caroline.

                    MAGGIE
It was Will Bannerman and André LeRoux. He knows we want the
same spot. I hope you can run in those shoes.

                    CAROLINE
I'll do it, don't worry about me.

                              Caroline and Maggie run off. The music from the
                              bush party starts up as they chase each other and
                              sing. Finally the music calms down a bit.

24 **EXT. GOLDFIELD/FOREST - PEARL AND JOHN GO INTO THE WOODS**

                              A light comes up on the other side of the stage
                              revealing John and Pearl who are crouching on the
                              ground looking at a bag full of "prospecting gear."
                              John looks cautiously around.

                    JOHN
Are we done then? My mom has been watching me all afternoon, I
couldn't get away. I was lucky to sneak off from the party. Let's go.

                    PEARL
Hang on. Just want to make sure that we be having everything is all.
Wouldn't want to be caught in the forest without. That's what my ma
always says.

JOHN
Well, if we don't get going, *my ma* will be the one we're going to deal with, Pearl.

> Pearl nods. They head into the forest, singing joyfully.

PEARL
THROUGH LAKES AND TREES AND ON THE BREEZE,

PEARL AND JOHN
WE'RE GOING ON AN ADVENTURE.

JOHN
AND I'LL BET YOU WE'LL FIND IT TOO

PEARL AND JOHN
FASTER THAN YOU CAN MEASURE.

THROUGH LAKES AND TREES AND ON THE BREEZE,
WE'RE GOING ON AN ADVENTURE.
AND I'LL BET YOU WE'LL FIND IT TOO
FASTER THAN YOU CAN MEASURE.

FOR GOLD,
WE KNOW,
WILL PUT US AT EASE.

OUR HEARTS,
WILL SHOW,
THE WAY TO GOLDEN SPLENDOR.

THE GOLD,
IT FLOWS,
THROUGH ROCK AT OUR FEET.

YOU'LL SEE,
IT GLOWS,
WAITING FOR US TO CAPTURE.

> Pearl and John start to skip off into the woods.

PEARL
THROUGH LAKES AND TREES

                    JOHN
AND ON THE BREEZE,

                PEARL AND JOHN
WE'RE GOING ON AN ADVENTURE.

                    PEARL
AND I'LL BET YOU

                    JOHN
WE'LL FIND IT TOO,

                PEARL AND JOHN
FASTER THAN YOU CAN MEASURE.

> Pearl and John go over a hill.

25 **EXT. GOLDFIELD/FOREST - RACE FOR THE PLOT/DANCE PARTY-MUSIC, DANCE , SINGING**

> On the other side of the stage Caroline and Maggie fight their way through the bush.

                    CAROLINE
CHANGE MY LIFE TONIGHT, OH GOLD!
I WILL HOLD YOU IN MY HANDS.
CHANGE ME BEFORE I GROW OLD.
BRING ME TO LIFE.
I'LL RUN ON, EVER ON, I DON'T CARE.
ONE MORE NIGHT.

> In the background the chorus arrives carrying sticks and building the fire for the party. There is a dangerous tension in the air as they sing a wordless tune under the lead's song.

                    MAGGIE
CHANGE MY LIFE TONIGHT, OH GOLD.
HURRY, KEEP MOVING, DON'T YOU LOOK BACK.
DON'T LOOK, THERE'S MEMORY HAUNTING THE TREES.

NEVER AGAIN I'LL HOLD YOU IN MY ARMS.
THE WORLD MOVES ON, RUNNING ON, SO WE RUN ON...

                    CAROLINE
SO WE RUN ON...

CAROLINE AND MAGGIE
FOR GOLD!

MAGGIE
WATCH YOUR STEP!
THESE TIMES BRING DANGER.
THE EARTH MUST HEAR OUR HUNGER!
KEEP MOVING ON.

CHANGE MY LIFE TONIGHT, OH GOLD!
BRING ME TO LIFE.
WORLD MOVES ON, I RUN ON, RUNNING ON.
ONE MORE NIGHT.

> Maggie leads Caroline over a hill. Will and André come in from the other side of the stage.

WILL
JUST A LITTLE GOLD WILL SEE US THROUGH.
ONE MORE NIGHT, I'LL COME BACK WITH...

ANDRÉ AND WILL
GOLD!

ANDRÉ
GOLD I WILL HAVE YOU COME SET ME FREE.
THROUGH THIS ANCIENT FOREST,
JUST A LITTLE MORE TO...

ANDRÉ AND WILL
GOLD!

> André and Will go off stage as the bush party becomes wild. The cultures try to "one-up" each other. The beats turn into a chant as the flames of the fire (represented by ribbons) grow higher.
>
> At last the chorus breaks into a full chant as Maggie and Caroline, André and Will run on to opposite sides of the stage.

MAGGIE
Just a little farther, watch your step.

CHORUS
Chip and block, flake and rock, plot and stock, you are mine.
Chip and block, flake and rock, plot and stock, you are mine.
Chip and block, flake and rock, plot and stock, you are mine.
Chip and block, flake and rock, plot and stock, you are all mine!

CAROLINE
JUST A LITTLE MORE.

WILL
JUST A LITTLE FARTHER, GLAD YOU'VE KEPT YOUR WAY!

MAGGIE, CAROLINE, ANDRÉ, WILL
ALL THE WAY TO GOLD!

ANDRÉ
GOLD! MY FUTURE! I HAVE IT IN MY HANDS!

Maggie and Caroline, Will and André come over the hill at the same moment. They all realize that they are at the gold site. Maggie passes Caroline the staking spikes. Will passes his spikes to André. The race is on to center stage to see who can stake the land first.

ALL
GOLD!

The fire at the bush party rages.

Both Caroline and André plant their spikes at exactly the same moment. Then the flames at the bush party surge out of control!

Thankfully, Pastor Schwidder sees. He douses the fire with water.

PASTOR SCHWIDDER
STOP!

As though a spell has been broken the bush party families look at each other, stunned as the lights go down.

Caroline, Maggie, André and Will stare at each other. This has never really happened before: two people spiking the same spot at exactly the same moment! The lights go down on them glaring at each other.

Act Two

ACT 2

> As the act opens and the set is revealed music plays from the campfire scene. It dies away and then...

26 **EXT. GOLDFIELD/FOREST - JOHN AND PEARL GET LOST- SONG**

> John and Pearl enter the woods, they are having a great old time. John hands Pearl a large golden rock. Pearl happily dances with it. They laugh. Dancers dressed as trees stand with their backs to the audience, John and Pearl dance around them.

          PEARL AND JOHN
THROUGH LAKES AND TREES AND ON THE BREEZE,
WE'RE GOING ON ADVENTURE.
AND I'LL BET YOU WE'LL FIND IT TOO,
FASTER THAN YOU CAN MEASURE.

THROUGH LAKES AND TREES AND ON THE BREEZE,
WE'RE GOING ON ADVENTURE.
AND I'LL BET YOU WE'LL FIND IT TOO,
FASTER THAN YOU CAN MEASURE.

FOR GOLD,
WE KNOW,
WILL PUT US AT EASE.
OUR HEARTS,
WILL SHOW,
THE WAY TO GOLDEN SPLENDOR.

THE GOLD,
IT FLOWS,
THROUGH ROCKS AT OUR FEET.
YOU'LL SEE,
IT GLOWS,
WAITING FOR US TO CAPTURE.

> Pearl and John start to play tag around a tree, forgetting to watch where they are going. The sky begins to grow dim.

          PEARL
THROUGH LAKES AND TREES,

JOHN
AND ON THE BREEZE,

PEARL AND JOHN
WE'RE GOING ON ADVENTURE.

PEARL
AND I'LL BET YOU,

PEARL AND JOHN
WE'LL FIND IT TOO, FASTER THAN YOU CAN MEASURE.

> Pearl stops where she is, noticing that they are lost and that it has become dark. John still sings and plays.

JOHN
AND I'LL BET YOU, WE'LL FIND IT TOO...

> Pearl tugs on John's arm. John stops dancing.

PEARL AND JOHN
AND I'LL BET YOU WE'LL FIND IT TOO.
AND I'LL BET YOU WE'LL FIND IT TOO...

> They look at each other in fear. The tune finishes on a sinister note. The trees turn, revealing that they are alive as John and Pearl watch. Holding hands, they run away further into the forest.

27 **EXT. GOLDFIELD/FOREST - CAROLINE AND ANDRÉ ROMANCE**

> Caroline and André are left alone. Caroline is desperately thirsty but she stubbornly licks her lips. She can't get to her water bag without moving off her spot. She stretches for it, leaving her toe on the edge of her staked area but can't reach her water. She sits back in her spot, folding her arms in frustration, moistening her lips again.

ANDRÉ
I'm not going to steal your spot if you get up to get your water.

CAROLINE
No thanks. I'm fine. I'm not moving an inch until Maggie gets back.

ANDRÉ
You can do as you like but Will and Maggie are going to be a while. They have to find an assayer, and that's hard enough without a party going on.

CAROLINE
In case you can't tell, I don't trust you.

ANDRÉ
That hurts.

CAROLINE
I staked this land first, you'll see. I will not move an inch until the proper authority settles this claim. I hope you are ready to pay up and get on the next train out of here.

ANDRÉ
Suit yourself. It's been hot all day, you ran all the way here, you can go get a drink.

CAROLINE
I'm fine.

ANDRÉ
I'm not heartless, you know. I'm not a cheater either.

CAROLINE
I'm not thirsty, really.

> André drinks some water. Caroline watches him out of the corner of her eye, she tries to moisten her dry lips. André catches her watching him. Smiling, he fans himself with his hat, making a big deal out of the heat.

ANDRÉ
Whew! It's hot this summer! There wasn't much snow this last winter either, although I imagine down in New York you wouldn't have heard about that. Not much water around these days.

> Caroline glares at him.

André (cont'd)
Yes sir, everything is dry, dry, dry.

> He takes another drink of water.

> Caroline scowls. André smiles at her, carelessly splashing water on his face. He takes some pork roll out of his sack and begins to eat it. Caroline can't help but watch. André smiles at her.

André (cont'd)
Oh sorry. Are you hungry too?

> André takes another swig of his water. Caroline bites her lip harder and turns away. André shakes his head.

André (cont'd)
Look, you are one tough lady, I'll give you that. You must be thirsty though. If you won't go and get your own water, take some of mine. Here, take a drink.

> He offers her his water. Caroline ignores him.

André (cont'd)
Take a drink. I don't want to have to carry you out of here if you faint. Please?

> Caroline regards him cautiously then takes a drink from his container.

CAROLINE
Thank you. (Pause) That's very nice of you.

ANDRÉ
You have no idea. How did a woman like you end up here anyway?

> He hands her some of the pork roll. Caroline takes it gratefully.

CAROLINE
(Laughs) Desperation and a big dream! Isn't that the same story as everyone else up here?

ANDRÉ
I guess so, but I've never met another lady prospector. You must be the most desperate woman in the world!

CAROLINE
Ha, ha. Just a big dreamer, that's all.

ANDRÉ
You must have done something before you decided to come here. Let me see... You are the heiress to a great fortune... After all, that's the right kind of dress.

CAROLINE
(Laughs again) It would be nice to be an heiress. The dress is from my aunt. This one was fashionable last year.

> Caroline adopts a dramatic pose.

CAROLINE (cont'd)
Ladies and Gentlemen! May I present, the toast of 1910! My uncle is a senator in Washington, where the fashion changes with the season, or with the opinion of the ladies auxiliary.

ANDRÉ
You're at least a year or two ahead up here I'd say. I'm not sure when it will be the fashion for women to wear a full gown and pistols in the bush.

> Caroline laughs and poses again.

CAROLINE
Why, thank you. For a poor relation it is good to be ahead of something, somewhere.

ANDRÉ
So, if you aren't rich then what did you do before you became a prospector? Governess?

CAROLINE
No.

ANDRÉ
You look too soft to be a maid.

CAROLINE
Do I? You don't think I'm strong?

ANDRÉ
You've never done hard work before, I can tell.

CAROLINE
Well, come here, give me your hand.

> Caroline shakes his hand, hard. André grimaces with pain.

ANDRÉ
Ouch. You didn't have to squeeze so hard.

CAROLINE
Do you give in then?

ANDRÉ
Oui.

> He catches her hand as she releases it.

André (cont'd)
Just a second. How are your fingers so strong when your hand isn't rough?

> He turns her hand over.

CAROLINE
You can't guess?

ANDRÉ
No, no, I've got it. Pastry maker?

CAROLINE
No.

ANDRÉ
Bookbinder. Flipping pages a lot.

CAROLINE
No.

ANDRÉ
You're an acrobat in the circus who walks only on her fingertips?

> Caroline laughs.

CAROLINE
No, of course not... I'm a pianist. A piano player.

ANDRÉ
Well, you're right, I would never have guessed that.

CAROLINE
I'm going to be a concert pianist too. My aunt used to have me play at her parties: Waltzes, art music, all kinds of things. My aunt likes to show me off. That's how I ended up with all these impractical dresses. I'm a real charity case.

ANDRÉ
I wouldn't worry about your clothes, you look... very nice. Before I left Montreal I used to watch all the rich people walk off the gangplank at Quai Russel and board the Grand Trunk line. Fashion is not very practical. You should have seen the ladies with big ostrich feather hats try to squeeze through the doors!

> Caroline laughs and then sighs.

CAROLINE
Thankfully there are a lot of important people at my uncle's parties. I have been offered a place with a famous teacher... in Paris, Rafael Joseffy. I just have to find the money to get to Paris. And then, I'll have my shot at playing piano in the big concert halls.

ANDRÉ
Rafael Joseffy? I've heard of him! I think I saw his name in the paper. There was a big to-do when he got off the train in New York. It was a lot of commotion over a music teacher.

CAROLINE
He's not just a teacher! He is *the* best Bach piano soloist in the world! He was probably in New York to play with the New York Philharmonic Orchestra. I wish I could play at that level... maybe someday, I hope someday.

ANDRÉ
Wow, you must be something.

CAROLINE
I'd like to be something. But I won't be anything unless I get a shot, and to get a shot, to get the training, I need money. The only way to get money and fast these days, that I'm willing to do, is to look for gold. So here I am! I've just got to get to Paris.

ANDRÉ
You sure aren't a regular woman.

CAROLINE
What is that supposed to mean?

ANDRÉ
Nothing, it's a compliment. I've never met anyone like you; you've got guts... you're kind of stupid to be coming straight into danger, but guts, you know.

CAROLINE
Thanks. How about you?

ANDRÉ
Oh, I'm just a poor kid from the Montreal docks. I've always been too poor to go to a concert.

CAROLINE
You've never been to a concert hall?

ANDRÉ
No never.

CAROLINE
Then you haven't lived. It is so quiet there, so full of life. I love everything about it. The smell of the wood and the rosin from the bows, the gas lights, the curtains. I even like the way the curtains smell, they are usually a little musty, like they haven't been cleaned since Mozart. I love the way your steps echo as you cross the boards, and your heart pounds. If you're lucky, you're there to play, and back stage behind the velvet curtains you can hear everyone rustling in the darkness, breathing, waiting. If I had the chance I know just what I would play too.

ANDRÉ
What's that?

CAROLINE
Brahms Piano Trio in B Major, the allegro.

ANDRÉ
Never heard of it.

CAROLINE
Never?

                    ANDRÉ
No.

                    CAROLINE
Oh, well then, you must hear it. Imagine, a great hall...

> Caroline gestures as though showing a great
> concert hall. As though he has stepped from her
> imagination, an elegantly dressed stage hand brings
> on chairs and stands. He dusts them off as
> Caroline watches.

                    CAROLINE (cont'd)
...To hear it best it must be a great one, a beautiful grand piano, shiny black and marvellous, full of golden wood and smooth white keys. There would be a couple of chairs.

> Caroline arranges the chairs.

                    CAROLINE (cont'd)
This trio is played with a cello and violin of course. Two music stands for them.

> Two musicians come on with their instruments and
> begin setting themselves up.

                    CAROLINE (cont'd)
My glorious white pages rustling in my hands, because I'm nervous, see? You are always nervous before you go on. It can't be helped but that's part of the excitement. You hear your name, the audience applauds. The moment comes faster than you planned, but every second after that is slower, like swimming underwater. This is it.

28 **INT. IMAGINARY CONCERT HALL - CAROLINE'S CONCERT**

                    CAROLINE
THE FIRST NOTE SO SWEETLY FALLS ON THE KEYS,
JOINED BY ITS FELLOW HUSHED HARMONY.
SOFTLY IT MEETS A COMPELLING THEME,
AND OH HOW MY HEART BEATS,
OH HOW THE KEYS SPEAK,
AND NOW THEY SEE THE PIANO GLEAM.

THE VIOLIN JOINS US AS WE SOAR IN THE AIR.
THE MUSIC'S SWEET MELODY FLOWS LIGHTLY EVERYWHERE.
NOW IT'S MY TURN TO FLY,

I WISH THE WORLD GOODBYE,
THE SWEETEST SIGH,
I JOIN THE SKY.

THE GREATEST ADVENTURE THAT YOU EVER COULD KNOW,
SITTING STILL IN YOUR CHAIR,
WITH EVERYWHERE,
AND ANYWHERE,
AND EVERYWHERE TO GO!
HOW I WILL FLY!
I'LL TAKE YOU TO THE SKY!
WHEN I PLAY,
DUM, DUM, DUM DUM.

     ANDRÉ

WHEN YOU PLAY.

     CAROLINE

DUM, DUM, DUM, DUM.
THAT'S WHAT A CONCERT,
THAT'S WHAT CONCERT,
THAT WHAT A CONCERT…

     ANDRÉ

HEAR THE SWEET MUSIC.

     CAROLINE

A CONCERT CAN BE!

     ANDRÉ AND CAROLINE

CAN BE, CAN BE

     CAROLINE

DA, DA, DA BABA DUM, DA, DA, DA BABA DUM
DUM, DUM, DUM, DUM DUM

> Caroline imitates the piano and André joins in copying her playfully with more and more enjoyment.

     CAROLINE (cont'd)

STILL AS A WHISPER MUSIC PLAYS ON,
HEART BEATING OUT THE NOTES OF THE SONG.

ANDRÉ AND CAROLINE
HERE IN THIS ROOM BEAUTY WALKS, I SEE.
MAKING OUR THOUGHTS GREET,
FEEL HOW OUR HEARTS MEET,
MUSIC CALLS US TO BE FREE!

HERE IN A CONCERT YOU ARE NEVER ALONE.
THE WORLD SITS IN DARKNESS, AS STARS CROWD AROUND YOUR HOME.

CAROLINE
THOUGH THE SWEET MOMENT FLIES,

ANDRÉ AND CAROLINE
WE'LL HOLD IT ALL OUR LIVES,

CAROLINE
THOUGH TIME GOES BY,

ANDRÉ AND CAROLINE
THIS SONG SURVIVES.

CAROLINE
THAT'S WHAT A CONCERT...

ANDRÉ
THAT'S WHAT A CONCERT...

ANDRÉ AND CAROLINE
THAT'S WHAT A CONCERT,
CAN BE!

ANDRÉ
I had no idea; are concerts really that wonderful?

CAROLINE
When the music is good and the musicians play with everything they have in them, then yes. Sometimes it's better than wonderful. Sometimes it's magic.

ANDRÉ
Would you take me?

Caroline turns to look at André.

CAROLINE
Of course. Yes, I would.

André smiles.

ANDRÉ
I would like that a lot.

CAROLINE
It's a shame they are all so far away. Mr.Joseffy gave me a brochure for one of the big concert halls they are building in Paris.

Caroline pulls out a brochure from her pocket. She tries to read it but completely mispronounces the french words.

CAROLINE (cont'd)
He said that one day, if I work hard, I might be one of the first soloists to play in a place like this, the Théâtre des Champs-Élysées.

ANDRÉ
Champs-Élysées. Yes. It looks wonderful.

Caroline mispronounces all the french words.

CAROLINE
Champs-Élyées. Oh look, see I think they are describing it here: Le Théâtre des Champs-Élysées est sans conteste l'un des...

ANDRÉ
... Des plus beaux...

CAROLINE
Théâtre des Champs-Élysées... Lieux de spectacle parisiens.

ANDRÉ
For a girl who is planning on going to France, your french is pretty terrible.

CAROLINE
Is it that bad? I really don't know what I'm saying.

ANDRÉ
Well... you could use some help. I could teach you a few words, important ones, so that you can find your way to the concert hall.

CAROLINE
Could you? Oh, that would be wonderful.

ANDRÉ
I've never been to Paris.

CAROLINE
They say it is beautiful.

ANDRÉ
I'm sure it is.

> They fall silent, looking at each other.

CAROLINE
I don't think I could find my way alone. My french is really bad.

ANDRÉ
Vous avez besoin de quelqu'un pour vous aider.

CAROLINE
Exactly.

ANDRÉ
You know, it is my dream to drive the fastest train in the world. It might be a good idea to go to Paris, to get some experience. I could help you with your French. Ce serait mon plaisir Madamoiselle...

> Caroline curtsies to him.

CAROLINE
Ma pleasure, Madamoiselle.

> André points to himself.

ANDRÉ
Monsieur.

CAROLINE
Montser.

> André takes her hand and uses it to point to himself.

ANDRÉ
Monsieur.

> Caroline shyly slips her hand away.

CAROLINE

Right. Monsieur.

They sing.

29 **EXT. GOLDFIELD/FOREST - ANDRÉ AND CAROLINE LOVE SONG (FRENCH LYRICS BY LUC MARTIN)**

ANDRÉ
SOUS LA TOILE DES ÉTOILES SCINTILLANTES,

CAROLINE
SEE THEM SHINE, SO STILL AND BRIGHT.

ANDRÉ
POUR NOUS DEUX, UN SPECTACLE D'AMOUREUX.

CAROLINE
TURNING MAGIC INTO NIGHT.

ANDRÉ
SOUS LA LUNE TOUT PRÈS DE MOI,

CAROLINE
KEEP ME SAFELY THERE ALL THROUGH THE NIGHT.

ANDRÉ
WHILE THE MOON ABOVE SHINES GOLDEN LIGHT,

CAROLINE
GOLDEN LIGHT, I'M HERE WITH YOU TONIGHT.
SPEAK YOUR WORDS TO ME,
MY HEART KNOWS THEM WELL.
I HEAR EVERY THOUGHT,
YOUR WORDS MEAN TO TELL.

ANDRÉ
DANS MON COEUR, LE DESTIN DE MES RÊVES.

CAROLINE
I HAVE DREAMED OF MOON-LIT NIGHTS,

ANDRÉ
DANS MON COEUR, JE VEUX TE RACONTER,

CAROLINE
WHEN THE WORLD IS LOST FROM SIGHT.

ANDRÉ
SOUS LA LUNE TOUT PRÈS DE MOI,

CAROLINE
KEEP ME SAFELY THERE ALL THROUGH THE NIGHT.

ANDRÉ
FOR A LOVE LIKE YOURS, I'D

ANDRÉ AND CAROLINE
GIVE ALL I HAVE
TO KNOW YOU ALL OF MY LIFE.

TES PENSEES ME SONT CHERES,
MY HEART KNOWS THEM WELL.
J'ENTENDS TA DOUCE TENDRESSE,
YOUR WORDS MEAN TO TELL.

ANDRÉ
SI JE T'OUVRE LA PORTE DE MON COEUR.

CAROLINE
IN YOUR HEART MY HEART WILL LIVE.

ANDRÉ
DANS LA JOIE, JE SERAI PRÈS DE TOI,

CAROLINE
YOU ALONE MYSELF I GIVE.

ANDRÉ
SOUS LA LUNE TOUT PRÈS DE MOI.

CAROLINE
KEEP ME SAFELY THERE ALL THROUGH THE NIGHT.

ANDRÉ
OUR DREAMS WILL FIND ONE WORLD ONE

ANDRÉ AND CAROLINE
WORLD, ONE HOPE
ONE HEART FOR ALL OF OUR LIFE.

TES PENSEES ME SONT CHERES,
MON COEUR RESSENT TA JOIE.

J'ENTENDS LA DOUCE TENDRESSE.
MON COEUR S'UNIT A TOI.

SPEAK YOUR WORDS TO ME,
MY HEART KNOWS THEM WELL.
I HEAR EVERY THOUGHT,
YOUR WORDS MEAN TO TELL.
(WHEN YOU) SPEAK YOUR WORDS TO ME,
(FOR MY) HEART WILL LISTEN WELL.

> André and Caroline stare at each other for a long moment. It seems all will be well.

30   EXT. GOLDFIELD/FOREST - FRANK'S VERSION OF HAPPINESS - SONG

> People are "sleeping it off" in the bush after the fire. Some families are drifting home. Others sit fanning themselves because of the heat. A few musicians still pluck absently on their instruments. The music slowly turns into "Come on, Come on."
>
> Frank is up to no good. He is prowling the sleepy crowd, "rolling drunks" for change while no one is looking. Maggie and Will enter.

FRANK
COME ON, COME ON TO THE PORCUPINE
WHERE THE STREETS ARE MADE OF GOLD!
PACK UP YOUR THINGS LEAVE YOUR CARES BEHIND,
BY TONIGHT I'LL HAVE WEALTH UNTOLD!

FOR I'M A ONE, I'M THE ONE, AND A SMART ONE TOO!
SUCH A THING'S NOT EASY TO DO!
JUST WAIT AND SEE IT WILL COME TO ME,
FOR I KNOW I DESERVE IT TOO!

> The music continues as Maggie and Will speak.

MAGGIE
Look, there's an assayer now.

> Will tries to hold Maggie back.

WILL
I don't trust him. There was some business over a land claim...

MAGGIE
You don't trust him? I don't trust you! Well, here's our assayer.

> Maggie walks over to Frank and picks him up by his collar. Frank is startled. He pretends that he is helping "tuck in" the drunks that he has been rolling over.

WILL
Maggie, I...

FRANK
COME ON, COME ON TO THE PORCUPINE,
WHERE THE STREETS ARE MADE OF GOLD!

MAGGIE
Never mind that, Frank. We need you.

FRANK
PACK UP YOUR THINGS, LEAVE YOUR CARES BEHIND, BY TONIGHT WE'LL HAVE WEALTH UNTOLD.

MAGGIE
We found gold.

> Frank looks astonished and greedily takes both their hands.

FRANK
FOR I'M A ONE, YOU'RE A ONE AND WE THREE WILL BE,
SOON TO MAKE OUR DREAMING COME TRUE.
COME ON, COME ON, WE'VE GOT GOLD TO FIND!
BID OUR WORRIES AND CARES ADIEU.
COME ON, COME ON, WE'VE GOT GOLD TO FIND!
BID OUR WORRIES AND CARES ADIEU!

> Will, frustrated with Frank's behaviour and the situation, pulls him to a stop.

WILL
Never mind that Frank. You just listen. We have... a situation.

                    MAGGIE
Our prospectors have staked the same land,

                    WILL
At the same time.

                    FRANK
That's not possible. Now, if you'll excuse me...

                    MAGGIE
It happened.

                    WILL
It's true Frank. Never thought I'd see it.

                              Frank studies them with new interest.

                    FRANK
Then there's a question of ownership?

                    WILL
That's right.

                    FRANK
And you need me to figure out who gets what?

                    WILL
We need an assayer.

                              Frank smiles slyly and eagerly shakes their hands.

                    FRANK
I'm your man. Just let me collect my things.

                              Frank moves off. Will follows after him.

                    MAGGIE
We'll have it settled tonight. Where are you going?

                    WILL
I don't trust him. He's not leaving my sight.

31 **GOLDFIELD/FOREST- THE MOTHERS LOOK FOR THEIR CHILDREN**

                              Mrs.Campsall looks through the crowd, waking
                              people up and talking to a few mothers who are
                              still awake.

> Coming from the other direction Mrs.O'Day, holding a piece of paper in her hand and still labouring with a headache, stops people too. Mrs.Campsall stops Maggie with obvious relief; Maggie always knows where the children are.

MRS.CAMPSALL
Have you seen my son?

MAGGIE
No, I'm sorry I haven't. You've lost him?

MRS.CAMPSALL
Again. He was supposed to be here but in all the commotion he's disappeared. That boy is going to give his mama a heart attack. He's about this tall, dark hair...

MAGGIE
I know John Campsall. I sent him home to you this morning.

MRS.CAMPSALL
He's gone again, and now it's dark what with the bears and the fires... Maggie, you're good at tracking things. Could you help me find him?

MAGGIE
John is a capable boy. You'll find him. I have something important to do tonight.

MRS.CAMPSALL
Oh, alright then.

MRS.O'DAY
Pearl! Where are you girl?

> Mrs.Campsall turns towards Mrs.O'Day. As soon as they see each other, they know what has happened. Maggie can't help but watch even though she is still trying to wait for Frank and Will.

MRS.O'DAY (cont'd)
Oh no! Not again.

MRS.CAMPSALL
So, you think my son and your daughter have run off together?

MRS.O'DAY

I'm most certain. Look here.

MRS.CAMPSALL

It looks like a list.

MRS.O'DAY

It's my daughter's. I found it lying about on the table. She always has a plan, that one. It seems she'd be looking for gold. Some of this here is not from my house, and your son is missing... she'd not be doing it alone if I know her.

MRS.CAMPSALL

Was she planning this for a while?

MRS.O'DAY

Not likely. She's a planner but a poor one with secrets. She'll keep her head.

> Maggie takes a step forward to intervene but changes her mind.

MRS.CAMPSALL

I should have never let him out of my sight. If anything happens to them... the bears are so hungry these days since the berries died in the heat... oh, the heat, he'll dehydrate, never had much sense... And the fires.

MRS.O'DAY

No good to worry, Abigail. We'll find them. At least, if I had any idea where to begin in the dark.

> Mrs.O'Day squeezes Mrs.Campsall's hands reassuringly but you can tell they are both scared and don't know what to do.

MAGGIE

I would start to the north, on the bush trail. The kids play there, they'd start where they know.

> The mothers have forgotten that Maggie was there.

MRS.O'DAY

Oh. Thank you.

> They look confusedly towards the bush, trying to decide where north is.

          MRS.CAMPSALL
North, you say?

          MRS.O'DAY
Oh, Pearl, my Pearl.

> Maggie watches them. She looks back in the direction of Will and Frank, trying to decide what to do. Finally...

          MAGGIE
I'll help you.

          MRS.O'DAY
Thank you, oh, thank you Maggie.

          MRS.CAMPSALL
You're a good woman Maggie Buffalo.

          MAGGIE
A mother is no mother with a broken heart.

> Maggie leads the women off the other direction.

32 EXT. GOLDFIELD/FOREST - THANK GOD FOR MOTHERS -SONG

> Pearl and John wander through the forest, afraid.

          PEARL
WHEN I WAS AFRAID
MY MOTHER STAYED
CLOSE TO MY BED.

          JOHN
WHILE I WOULD SLEEP
HER WATCH WOULD KEEP
TOUCHING MY HEAD.

          PEARL AND JOHN
WHERE WERE THE MONSTERS
WHO DARED TO STEAL ME
FROM MOTHER'S ARMS?

IF I WERE BACK NOW,
I DON'T CARE HOW,
I'D STAY IN HER ARMS.

MOTHER I'M COMING HOME.
MOTHER I'M COMING HOME!

>   Mrs.Campsall, Mrs.O'Day follow Maggie through the woods. Maggie stops every now and then as though she has seen an important sign.

MRS.CAMPSALL
WHEN HE WAS YOUNG
I KNEW IT ALL
I WAS HIS SKY.

MAGGIE
SOMETIMES THINGS CHANGE
YOU CAN'T EXPLAIN
NEVER A WHY.

MRS.CAMPSALL, MRS.O'DAY
WHERE WERE THE MONSTERS
WHO DARED TO STEAL THEM
FROM STRONG, LOVING ARMS?

IF THEY WERE BACK NOW,
I DON'T CARE HOW,
THEY'D STAY IN MY ARMS.

CHILDREN PLEASE COME BACK HOME.
CHILDREN PLEASE COME BACK HOME!

MAGGIE
WINTER FORGETS THE SUN
MEMORY GOES ON AND ON.

WHAT WOULD I GIVE? EVERYTHING AND FOREVER.
MY HEART GOES ON WITHOUT THEIR CALL.
THOUGH DARKNESS COMES AND FEAR FOLLOWS SOFTLY AFTER,
WE'LL STRUGGLE ON THROUGH NIGHT-TIME'S FALL.

> John puts his arm around Pearl protectively, even though he is the scared one.

                    MRS.CAMPSALL, MRS.O'DAY AND MAGGIE

COME BACK TO ME,
FOLLOW MY VOICE,
COME BACK HOME!

COME BACK TO ME,
MY VOICE WILL LEAD,
FOLLOW IT HOME!

SAFE FROM THE MONSTERS
WHO WANT TO STEAL YOU
AWAY FROM MY ARMS.

I NEED YOU BACK NOW,
I DON'T CARE HOW,
PLEASE COME TO MY ARMS.

                    PEARL AND JOHN

I'M COMING HOME.
I'M COMING HOME.
PLEASE OPEN YOUR ARMS.

                    MRS.CAMPSALL, MRS.O'DAY AND MAGGIE

LEAD THEM HOME.
LEAD THEM HOME.
LEAD THEM HOME.

                    PEARL AND JOHN

I'M COMING HOME.
I'M COMING HOME.
SO GOOD TO BE HOME.

> The two groups see each other. The children and Mrs.Campsall and Mrs.O'Day run towards each other but Maggie stops still, unable to go on. She begins to walk away.

                    MRS.O'DAY
Maggie, will you come?

> Maggie stares at the ground, she cannot watch.

MRS.O'DAY (cont'd)
Oh. I understand... You know Maggie, all mothers have broken hearts.

> Mrs.O'Day comes back and squeezes Maggie's hand.

MRS.O'DAY (cont'd)
Thank you. If there's ever anything I can do...

MAGGIE
Just love your children.

> Mrs.O'Day nods and squeezing her hand again she runs towards Pearl. Mrs.Campsall is already hugging John. Maggie watches for a minute then turns and leaves.
>
> Pearl and Mrs.O'Day embrace again. Mrs.Campsall cuffs John on the shoulder.

MRS.CAMPSALL
What on earth were you thinking young man?

JOHN
Well, I...

MRS.CAMPSALL
You have a lot of explaining to do. Do you have any idea what you've done to me? Dragged my heart nearly right out of my mouth you did. Right out of my mouth. Don't you dare do that again, do you hear me? Do you?

JOHN
Yes I, but...

MRS.CAMPSALL
Don't but me. There's no buts here. Not a one.

JOHN
But mom. We found something. Show her Pearl.

PEARL
Look ma, we found gold.

MRS. CAMPSALL
You were out here looking for rocks?! Why of all the incredible, self absorbed...

MRS. O'DAY
Do you think it is Pearl? Let me see it.

PEARL
I think it is ma. It looks like my books. And I saw some before, Mr. Bannerman showed me.

MRS. CAMPSALL
What's this?

JOHN
We found gold mom.

> Mrs. Campsall looks John over, a gleam of pride on her face.

MRS. CAMPSALL
John... John Campsall....

MRS. O'DAY
We'll take it to Frank the assayer, tomorrow morning. What do you say? If it is worth something we'll know then, but now let's get them home.

MRS. CAMPSALL
My John. Oh, you're a bother, but... let's get you home.

> Mrs. Campsall hugs John again. The mothers lead their children home.

33 EXT. GOLDFIELD/FOREST - FRANK CAN'T BE TRUSTED

> Caroline and André are where we left them. Frank the asseyer has arrived with Will, interrupting the romance.

FRANK
(Snickers) What have we here? I think we came back a little too soon.

ANDRÉ
Will!

FRANK
Oh, no need to explain, this sort of thing happens all the time out in the bush. It must be the air. Now, what seems to be the problem? I've been dragged from my bed all the way out here.

WILL
Dragged from your bed? If your bed was the forest floor, and your bed time snack a bottle of gin.

FRANK
I guess I just need to go then.

WILL
No, no, Frank, it was good of you to come.

FRANK
That's more like it.

CAROLINE
Where's Maggie?

WILL
Maggie will see you in the morning Caroline, some kids were lost in the woods, and she thought she'd help.

>Frank snorts.

FRANK
Probably a snack for some bear is my guess. Those women should keep better control of their children.

WILL
That's enough, Frank. Just do what you came to do.

FRANK
It's up to you. Where are the stakes?

>André takes Will aside while Caroline shows Frank the stakes.

ANDRÉ
What's Frank doing here? I thought you said he couldn't be trusted.

WILL
He can't! Maggie picked him, I tried to warn her but this gold business seems to knock the sense out of everyone, including her.

ANDRÉ
We'll have to watch him carefully.

WILL
What do you think I've been doing? I've got to get home to Christy though. She'll be worried. She's not used to this place yet.

ANDRÉ
Leave it to me Will.

WILL
You're a good guy, André.

> Caroline has led Frank over to where the stakes are. She points them out.

CAROLINE
Right here.

FRANK
You're a pretty little thing to be out in the woods. Too pretty to be eaten by a bear, that's for sure. How be you come on home with me? I'll treat you real nice, like a lady.

ANDRÉ
What are you doing? Don't you touch her.

WILL
We're just asking you to test the ground and make a ruling, Frank.

CAROLINE
I can take care of myself.

FRANK
Oh ho, I'm sure you can.

ANDRÉ
Leave her alone. She doesn't need any of your betise.

WILL
Take it easy André, it's just the drink talking. Look Frank, if you scuff the earth just here, it's good mineral.

FRANK
Humm. Maybe. You haven't cleared it much. I have to do everything myself, I guess.

> The others watch curiously as Frank piles some wood together on top of the rock. They are not sure what he's doing.

FRANK (cont'd)
I'll just get out my tinder and burn it away a little.

> He pulls his matches out of his pocket and starts to strike it.

ANDRÉ, WILL AND CAROLINE
No!

ANDRÉ
Es-tu Fou!

WILL
One stray spark and we'll have a real fire on our hands. It's way too dry to burn the scruff like normal.

FRANK
Have it your way. It will take a while to go through some samples.

ANDRÉ
And the stakes?

FRANK
I'll measure it out, and let you know.

WILL
You'll let us know.

FRANK
I'll let you know. It doesn't happen over night.

> André helps him measure and then watches him write it down. André continues to stand right over his shoulder watching him.

Frank (cont'd)
You can go home. I'll take it from here.

>   André and Will exchange looks. Will and Caroline
>   start to go off.

                WILL
Come on Caroline, it will be a while. I'll walk you home.

                CAROLINE
Thanks Will.

>   Caroline turns to Frank.

                CAROLINE (cont'd)
I want to hear about it in the morning though.

                FRANK
Oh, yes ma'm.

>   Frank smiles terribly. Caroline is out of ear shot
>   but André hears.

                FRANK (cont'd)
Maybe earlier than that.

                ANDRÉ
What are you up to, Frank?

>   Frank eyes him up innocently.

                FRANK
What do you mean?

                ANDRÉ
You know what I mean.

>   Frank shrugs and turns back to the rock, casually
>   scuffing it with his foot.

                FRANK
I don't know that this rock is worth anything at all. Doesn't look the sort that was born right, you know what I mean. Low class. Doesn't mix.

>   The comment was clearly made about André, not
>   the rock. André chooses to ignore it.

                ANDRÉ
That rock is perfectly good and you know it. I know it.

FRANK
Remains to be seen. Well, I'm almost done here. I think I'll go back and rent a room tonight.

ANDRÉ
What are you talking about?

FRANK
That nice hotel near the drug store. They have nice beds. Although, the locks on the doors were never that good, you just jiggle them a little and it opens right up. It's too bad the manager sleeps like a log. Not safe if you ask me, but then I'm not a woman so what do I care?

ANDRÉ
You wouldn't dare.

FRANK
What are you trying to say? I'm feeling sleepy that's all.

>André goes to fight him, but Frank holds up his notebook.

FRANK (cont'd)
Now, now, I'm all there is between you and this land. I wouldn't do that.

>André slowly brings his fist down.

ANDRÉ
You touch her... you even breathe near her and I guarantee you, I will finish this. You already have no one, and it won't be long until you have nothing. You're a fool.

>André grabs his stuff and runs off in the direction Caroline went.

FRANK
You do what's good for you... and I'll do what's best for me...

>Frank chuckles as he takes André's stake out of the ground. He starts to sing.

34 EXT. GOLDFIELD/FOREST - GOLD RUNS IN RIVERS THROUGH FINGERS THAT CAN

                    FRANK
TAKE CARE OF YOURSELF,
AND I'LL TAKE CARE OF ME.
FOLLOW CONSCIENCE, FOLLOW SWEETNESS,
AND GUESS JUST WHERE YOU'LL BE!

TAKE CARE OF YOURSELF!
BY FAR A BETTER PLAN.
SOON YOU'RE LIVING, LIKE YOU'RE DREAMING,
OTHERS ONLY WISH THEY CAN.

FOR GOLD RUNS DOWN IN RIVERS
BENEATH THE FEET THAT CAN.
YOU QUESTION WHO WILL TAKE THE CHANCES?
I WILL BE THAT MAN!

I CARE FOR MYSELF
AND WHO BEST TO CARE FOR ME?
TAKE A MOMENT TO ENVISION
MY LIFE AS IT SHOULD BE.

YOU CARE FOR YOURSELF
WHAT YOU NEED TO JUST GET BY.
THE GOOD BOOK SAYS "LOVE EACH OTHER"
BUT THE BEST WE DO IS LIE.

FOR GOLD RUNS DOWN IN RIVERS
BENEATH THE FEET THAT CAN.
YOU QUESTION WHO WILL TAKE THE CHANCES?
I WILL BE THAT MAN!

I WILL BE THAT MAN.
SHEER AUDACITY!
TAKING THE WORLD IN MY HANDS
AND EVERYONE WILL SEE!
I WILL BE,
ABLY,
CERTAINLY,
DELIVERING THE PLAN.
GOLD RUNS DOWN THE HILLS IN RIVERS
 I WILL FILL MY HANDS.

OH MOMMA YOU WILL KNOW
THAT I CAN BE A MAN!
YOU WILL SEE ME.
YOU'LL KNOW THAT I BELONG.

> Frank starts a "fire" on the ground. As he sings this next part small "flames" shoot up and lick the pile of wood. The flames are really orange and red ribbons that flutter and sway over the wood. One ribbon escapes from the wood fire. Unnoticed by Frank, it snakes along the ground and winds it's way around a nearby tree. The ribbon flame crawls around and around the tree. When it reaches the top, more flame ribbons burst from the top of the tree. A dancer dressed as a flame takes one of the ribbons from the tree and moves, the ribbon twirling all the time, to another tree, that tree bursts into flames as well and another dancer appears. This happens again and now there are three flame dancers on the stage.

FRANK (cont'd)
FOR GOLD RUNS DOWN IN RIVERS
BENEATH THE FEET THAT CAN.
YOU QUESTION WHO WILL TAKE THE CHANCES?
I WILL BE THAT MAN!

I WILL BE THAT MAN!

> The flames stare angrily at Frank, who is still triumphantly looking at his gold, and begin to close in on him. In horror Frank realizes he is surrounded by fire and can't escape. The flame dancers close in. He falls down on the ground. They pause for a moment and then cause the ribbons to dive down on him. Blackness.

35   **EXT. PORCUPINE CAMP - FIRE SEQUENCE STARTS: THE UNIMAGINABLE HAPPENS**

> It is morning, very hot. The town is waking up. Lillian is sweeping the walk in front of the store. Christie Bannerman comes by.

CHRISTY
Good morning, Lillian.

LILLIAN
Morning Christy. Kind of day you'd fry an egg on, don't you think?

CHRISTY
I didn't sleep a wink last night it was so hot.

LILLIAN
I don't like the smell of today. Don't like it at all. Is Will back from the bush yet?

CHRISTY
He came home early this morning, but he went right back in. He's being really cautious with his stake this time. Said something about not trusting Frank.

LILLIAN
There's something a little off with that man. I've seen his type before, more going on there than meets the eye. I'd not trust him either.

CHRISTY
Well, he's the asseyer they were able to find.

LILLIAN
Don't you worry none. Will's been here a long time, I'm sure he can take care of himself.

I don't like this day too well. It smells like fire, and Lord knows there's been far too many of those this summer.

CHRISTY
You don't think there would be another one today, do you?

LILLIAN
Well, I don't know. It seems as though the whole bush is gearing up for something.

CHRISTY
I hope he has the sense to come in, if there's fire. I made him promise.

LILLIAN
I don't know, lamb. I wouldn't worry yourself too much.

CHRISTY
Well, I'll keep an eye out all the same. I came in for some oil of cajeput. We're all out, and Jenny likes to have it on hand. You know how those men are, they're always getting hurt.

LILLIAN
Don't I know it. We have a few bottles left, come on in for a bit.

> Christy and Lillian go inside. While J.R. walks by with his towel. John Gauley enters.

JOHN GUALEY
Good morning J.R.. Off for a dip?

J.R.
Are you kidding? It's so hot I don't think I'll even need a towel to dry off. Why don't you join me?

JOHN GUALEY
Not today. I've got to get a few deliveries in before the heat really catches on. My mare's partial to sun-stroke.

J.R.
Suit yourself.

> J.R. looks off stage left.

J.R. (cont'd)
Would you look at that.

JOHN GUALEY
What? Oh!

J.R.
That is one big column of smoke. Take a look at those birds. What are those?

> The sound of birds crying fills the air.

JOHN GUALEY
Nighthawks.

J.R.
They're circling the whole thing, just screaming too.

JOHN GUALEY
That doesn't look good.

                    JOHN GUALEY
I think you had better cancel your swimming trip today, don't you?

                    J.R.
Yeah, that might be a good idea. Maybe I'll go back to the house, make sure everything is in order. Have you seen Will and André?

                    JOHN GUALEY
Nope. I hope to God they're not in the bush though. This just doesn't feel right.

>   Mrs.Campsall and John arrive carrying the rock.

                    JOHN GUALEY (cont'd)
Hey there, Mrs.Campsall!

                    MRS.CAMPSALL
Yes, Mr.Reid.

                    JOHN
How are the horses today, Mr.Reid?

                    JOHN GUALEY
They're fine John, just fine. Listen, I don't like the look of that smoke cloud over there.

                    MRS.CAMPSALL
My goodness, that's as big as I've seen all summer.

                    JOHN GUALEY
Bigger, I think. Listen, it's just my advice but I wouldn't wander around town today. I know you've got a little one at home and I'd hate to think what would happen in a fire with your children all alone. Is your husband home today?

                    MRS.CAMPSALL
No, he has gone into the bush to look for a claim. Myrtle is looking after little Robert. It looks as though the smoke is moving, doesn't it?

>   John Gualey pats John on the shoulder and begins
>   to move off.

JOHN GUALEY
Not saying it is, but just in case.

MRS.CAMPSALL
Yes. I see what you mean.

JOHN
Hey, Mr.Reid! Can I go riding with you today?

JOHN GUALEY
Not today John. Another time perhaps. You get on home with your mom, alright? No disappearing.

MRS.CAMPSALL
Come on John.

JOHN
But we were bringing our rock in today to see Fancy Frank... I mean the asseyer, you promised.

MRS.CAMPSALL
We'll do it again, John, another day.

JOHN
But we shouldn't wait. What if someone steals it?

MRS.CAMPSALL
Come on John, now!

> Mrs.Campsall and John start to go off as Christie and Lillian come out of the drug store.

CHRISTY
Thank you so much Lillian. Good morning Mrs.Campsall, John.

MRS.CAMPSALL
Good morning Christy, Lillian. I'd get on home now if I were you.

CHRISTY
Why is that?

LILLIAN
Oh my goodness gracious, mother Mary save us all!

> They all look offstage towards the fire. A wind has started blowing and they all react.

> Christy grabs for her hat. Perhaps the sign on the store starts to creak back and forth.

CHRISTY
Oh my. Oh no, Will!

> Christy bolts towards the bush, but Lillian holds her back.

LILLIAN
Now, don't you go doing anything foolish. Your Will has been up here since the start of the rush, he can take care of himself. But if he comes home and finds you gone, what is he going to do?

CHRISTY
I don't know.

LILLIAN
He'll go out of his mind, that's what. Now look at me. Take your eyes off that thing and look here. You're going to go to George's house, you were going to go there anyway, they'll take you to the lake. George and Jenny are very sensible, you listen to them. Now, I know there's a lady on your way, nine months pregnant, do you know her?

CHRISTY
Yes, I think I've met her.

LILLIAN
Well, her husband works at the mines. You just tell her to come down to me, will you? Can you do that job?

CHRISTY
Yes.

LILLIAN
Good. Now get on and quit staring.

MRS.CAMPSALL
You can come with us part way. Come on John, hurry on!

> Christy, Mr.Campsall and John leave just as John Gauley reappears. More people are starting to rush through town with blankets and belongings, away from the fire and towards the lake.

LILLIAN

Mr.Reid! John!

JOHN GUALEY

I can't stop now Lillian.

LILLIAN

It's just that I know the Campsall's will be looking for a horse.

JOHN GUALEY

I can't stop now! It's a fire alright, and a good one. Looks like it will be headed straight for the West Dome too. I'm going to try to get there ahead of it and get those people out.

LILLIAN

Lord bless ya, John. The almighty is coming I think.

36 **EXT. GOLDFIELD/FOREST - FIRE SEQUENCE: CAROLINE AND ANDRÉ AND THE FIRE**

> Maggie and Will meet in the bush.

MAGGIE

Will Bannerman? What are you doing up so early in the morning?

WILL

Just taking a walk, like yourself. Nice morning for it.

MAGGIE

(Laughs) Yes, nice morning. You couldn't sleep either?

WILL

Not a wink. I couldn't get my mind off the look in Frank's eyes. I don't trust him. I'm going to sit there right with him until he is done. No funny business, right?

MAGGIE

Good idea.

> Caroline and André arrive together. They are caught up in conversation but stop awkwardly as if caught when they see Will and Maggie.

CAROLINE

Hi.

ANDRÉ
Hi.

MAGGIE
Oh, you two are on speaking terms, are you? Well, at least we won't have to break up any fist fights.

WILL
From what I saw last night, I don't think that will be a problem. You two won't be forgetting about your bet, or about the deals you made, right André?

ANDRÉ
No. I haven't forgotten.

>Caroline steps away from André.

CAROLINE
Why of all the... I haven't forgotten either. I could use ten dollars. I will have to hire a good interpreter in France.

ANDRÉ
I didn't mean that...

CAROLINE
I don't like being made a fool of, especially by a man.

ANDRÉ
Is that so?

CAROLINE
Yes, that's so.

ANDRÉ
Well, you can think about that when I am using your ten dollars to buy my way as a Conductor. Upper class, the whole way.

CAROLINE
Well, I hope you will be happy.

ANDRÉ
I will be, no doubt about it.

>Maggie stops them.

WILL
What's wrong Maggie?

MAGGIE
The forest has gone quiet. Shh.

WILL
I hear it too.

MAGGIE
Something has spooked the animals.

CAROLINE
Like a bear?

MAGGIE
Oh no. Not a bear. It's as though the whole world has stopped speaking. Do you smell that Will?

WILL
No... Oh, yes.

Maggie and Will exchange looks.

ANDRÉ
I smell it too. The tops of the trees are moving, they're bending right over, the wind is so strong.

CAROLINE
What's going on?

MAGGIE
No time for questions Caroline. Can you run?

CAROLINE
I think so.

ANDRÉ
Good, take my hand.

Maggie leads the way, André and Caroline hold hands as they rush through the forest. Caroline needs help because she is still wearing those ridiculous boots. Maggie stops and waves everyone on.

37 **EXT. GOLDFIELD/FOREST - FIRE SEQUENCE: RUN DOWN TO THE WATER**

> MAGGIE

RUN DOWN TO THE WATER
HURRY ON, NO TIME FOR TURNING BACK.
THE WORLD IS A CHANGING
FALLING OFF OF ITS TRACKS.
RUN DOWN TO THE WATER,
RUN DOWN TO THE WATER!

> ANDRÉ

RUN DOWN TO THE WATER
DON'T GIVE IN!
YOUR LEGS ARE BURNING,
AND YOUR BREATH IS THIN!
RUN DOWN TO THE WATER, RUN DOWN TO THE WATER!

THOUGH THE DAY GROWS LONG
WE'RE RUNNING.
WE MUST CARRY ON
THOUGH IT'S FRIGHTENING.

DON'T LOSE HOPE, JUST REMEMBER,
JUST KEEP RUNNING DOWN,
DOWN TO THE WATER.

> MAGGIE

It's not much farther.

> The music increases and the fire, represented by dancers with rhythmic dancing ribbons begin to come out, "destroying" the trees as they go. Caroline stumbles.

> CAROLINE

Oh, these boots!

> André picks her up and takes her by the hand. André looks off stage.

> ANDRÉ

Oh no, Will! The train brought a load of dynamite in yesterday. That's the car there, look.

WILL
It's right in the path of the fire. Are you sure?

ANDRÉ
Of course I'm sure. I know everything about that train.

WILL
We can't do anything about it.

ANDRÉ
We have to. It's sitting right at the water's edge. Look at all those people Will. If it blows up where it is, no one will survive. I know how to move it but I can't do it alone.

CAROLINE
I'll help.

ANDRÉ
No!

CAROLINE
I'm as good as any man.

ANDRÉ
I know you are. Please.

WILL
Christy might be in there. Alright André, lead the way.

> Caroline holds on to André as he turns to go. He sings to her.

ANDRÉ
RUN DOWN TO THE WATER
HURRY ON, NO TIME FOR TURNING BACK.
THE WORLD, IS A CHANGING,
FALLING OFF ITS TRACKS.

> Will pulls André from Caroline.
>
> Maggie takes Caroline's hand and leads her on.

"Heart of Gold, The Musical" Kuhl & Martin

                          MAGGIE
DON'T STOP NOW
DON'T YOU DARE GIVE IN
RUN DOWN TO THE WATER
AND DIVE ON IN.
RUN DOWN TO THE WATER, RUN DOWN TO THE WATER!

38   **EXT. O'DAY HOUSE - FIRE SEQUENCE: THE O'DAY FAMILY, MAGGIE AND CAROLINE**

                                        Another piece of scenery moves, revealing Pearl and her mother who are sweeping the walk outside their house. Maggie and Caroline run in. Maggie sings.

                          MAGGIE
RUN DOWN TO THE WATER!

                                          Pearl's father, a kind, hard working man, wanders in with Charlie, Pearl's brother who is about 15.

                        MR.O'DAY
What's the trouble Maggie?

                          MAGGIE
A great wall of flame is coming.

Run down to the water!

                                          Mr.O'Day nods. The whole family gathers together and starts to run after Maggie and Caroline. Mr.O'Day stops suddenly. Maggie turns to watch.

                          PEARL
Papa!

                        MRS.O'DAY
What are you doing?

                        MR.O'DAY
I'm going to try to save the house. The lads will help to wet down the wood.

                        MRS.O'DAY
No! We can start again, come with us.

MR.O'DAY
It's too much money Fee (Fiona), we'd lose it all. I've got to try.

MRS.O'DAY
Then I'm staying with you.

MR.O'DAY
Look at me. Who is going to take our Pearl and Charlie?

CHARLIE
But Dad, you'll need me, I can help.

MR.O'DAY
No, the wind has whipped the water up high. Please, my boy?

> Mr.O'Day touches Mrs.O'Day's hair and lays a hand on Pearl. He shakes Charlie's hand. Mr.O'Day runs off. Maggie offers Mrs.O'Day her hand.

MAGGIE
Come with us, I know the way.

> Dropping her broom, Mrs.O'Day takes her children's hands and turns towards the river following Maggie.

39 FIRE SEQUENCE: RUN DOWN TO THE WATER

MRS.O'DAY
RUN DOWN TO THE WATER.
HURRY ON NO TIME FOR TURNING BACK
THE WORLD IS A CHANGING
FALLING OFF IT'S TRACKS.

> The Fire cuts the little group off surrounding them. Maggie quickly takes the group through a hidden door in the set.

MAGGIE AND CAROLINE
RUN DOWN TO THE WATER, RUN DOWN TO THE WATER!

40   EXT. PORCUPINE CAMP - FIRE SEQUENCE: THE CAMPSALLS

> The scene shifts again. John Campsall and his mother are with his brother(Samuel), sister (Myrtle) and a little baby (Robert.) Two older half sisters are with them (Sarah and Netta.)They have all their luggage around them and are huddled together.

MRS.CAMPSALL
Mr.Reid! Mr.Reid!

> J.R. Is running by with a bucket. He stops for a moment.

MRS.CAMPSALL (cont'd)
Of all the infernal things. He won't stop to help a woman in need!

J.R.
He hasn't stopped to take you?

MRS.CAMPSALL
Well, he did, but he wouldn't take any of our luggage until he was done. I am not moving until he does. Lord knows what people are like when the law disappears. And we have some... special cargo in one of these bags.

J.R.
With all due respect, it's no use ma'am. He has no time to take luggage, the world is burning up.

MRS.CAMPSALL
Well. Humph. Well. This is all we have.

J.R.
You have your children.

> Mrs.Campsall looks down at her children who are holding her legs, she suddenly holds them tightly as if snapping out of a dream. J.R. goes to move on. Mrs.Campsall looks around her in confusion.

MRS.CAMPSALL
I'm sorry, Mr.Andréws?

                    JR.
Yes?

                    MRS.CAMPSALL
What should I do?

                    J.R.
I think your best bet is to head down to Porcupine Lake with the rest of them.

                    MRS.CAMPSALL
Alright... Mr.Andréws?

                    J.R.
Yes?

                    MRS.CAMPSALL
Everything looks so... I can't seem to tell where we are there's so much smoke. Which way is the lake?

                    J.R.
This way.

>   Mrs.Campsall and her children start off towards the lake as J.R. runs off with his bucket.

                    MRS.CAMPSALL
RUN DOWN TO THE WATER. RUN DOWN TO THE WATER!

>   The flames start to surround them, dancing and dropping little sparks on the children's clothing. Mrs.Campsall pauses to brush them off periodically.

41 **EXT. DOME MINE - FIRE SEQUENCE: THE WEISS FAMILY**

>   The Weiss family and Dome crew come into view. Robert Weiss is helping Jeanna along, she is fussing with Ariel who is crying.

                    ROBERT WEISS
Come on now, Jeanna, bring Ariel.

                    JEANNA
She won't stop fussing. Shh, little Ariel, shh.

ROBERT WEISS
It will be alright. We'll go down the mine shaft until it's over, just like last time. Hurry!

JEANNA
It's like a wall, Robert. Have you ever seen a fire like that? It's as though it's alive.

ROBERT WEISS
Come on now.

> John Gualey Reid rushes on.

JOHN GUALEY
Hurry on, everyone. My mare is waiting, I'll take you on my cart. Hurry, the fire is headed this way.

ROBERT WEISS
Thank you kindly Mr.Reid but we'll be alright.

JOHN GUALEY
That's not a good idea. I've been all around this fire and it's bigger than anything I've ever seen. I've come to take you to the lake. Come on.

IRISH MINER
We will not fit, boy-o. Your cart is too small.

> John Gualey looks over at Robert Weiss. He's not going to fit.

JOHN GUALEY
No, not likely, but... I'll take you first Mrs.Weiss, and the baby, but come on, now.

UKRANIAN MINER
You are not going to get back in time.

JOHN GUALEY
I'll get back.

> Jeanna takes a step back towards Robert Weiss.

                    JOHN GUALEY (cont'd)
You can't go down the shaft, it will be the death of you. It's no ordinary fire.

                    JEANNA
The shaft will be fine.

                    ROBERT WEISS
Go on, all of you.

                    IRISH MINER
You need someone to man the pump.

                    UKRANIAN MINER
And some one to keep the cloths wet.

                    IRISH MINER
The shaft will do.

                    JOHN GUALEY
You're fools! All of you! Get on the cart!

                    No one moves.

                    JEANNA
Thank you kindly Mr.Reid.

                    John Gualey stares at them and shakes in frustration.

                    JOHN GUALEY
You can't say I didn't try.

                    John Gualey walks off. Robert Weiss shakes the hands of all the men. They begin to climb down the shaft followed by Jeanna and the baby.

42 **INT. DOME MINE SHAFT**

                    ROBERT WEISS
You should have gone my love.

                    JEANNA
But not without you.

                    ROBERT WEISS
Aren't you afraid?

JEANNA
WHEN I LOOK INTO YOUR EYES,

MEN'S CHORUS
WE WILL NEVER SAY GOODBYE,

JEANNA
I AM SURROUNDED BY

JEANNA AND MEN'S CHORUS
LOVE.
WHERE IS FEAR?

JEANNA
TAKE MY HAND REMEMBER DEAR,

MEN'S CHORUS
CLOSE MY EYES AND YOU ARE NEAR.

JEANNA
WE ARE SURROUNDED BY

JEANNA AND MEN'S CHORUS
LOVE.
WHERE IS FEAR?
OH, WHERE IS FEAR?

> They all sing their song which is calm. The miners take out the photos of their loved ones. Everyone settles themselves in the pit. It is then joined by the other groups on stage and the chaos returns. The waves grow higher the flames thicker, surrounding them all.

ROBERT WEISS
EVERYONE HOPES TO FIND THEIR FUTURE

ROBERT WEISS AND JEANNA
DIGGING DEEP IN HILLS OF GOLD.
THEY HOPE TO FIND THE ANSWER
IN WHAT IS BOUGHT AND SOLD.

                    ROBERT WEISS, JEANNA AND CHORUS
I WISH EVERY MOMENT
BRINGS LIFE WITH YOU TO SHARE
I'D TRADE THOSE GOLDEN HILLSIDES
TO FIND YOU WAITING THERE.

43   **EXT. PORCUPINE LAKE - FIRE SEQUENCE: THE DYNAMITE CAR EXPLODES**

                    Everyone except Will and André go into the "water." Maggie leads a group of women and children into the water. Caroline and Maggie help the children hold their heads above the waves. Mrs.Campsall and crew are joined at the edge of the lake by members of the chorus. They become desperate as they try to fight their way past "the flames" and stay in the "water." There is an explosion and the people in the water area fall down.

44   **EXT. PORCUPINE LAKE AND DOME MINE SHAFT - FIRE SEQUENCE: THE FIRE ENDS**

                    Time slows to a crawl. Names of the dead are listed. The people in the mine shaft all lay down. They are dead. People slowly begin to rise from the ground. Others bring in stretchers bearing their dead loved ones. Pastor Schwidder gives them the sign of the cross. The flames carry the bodies away.

                            VOICE OVER
A . Seircy McDonald , A. E. Burt and wife, A. J. Ryan, A. W. Dexter, A. W. Ross, Andréw Quesnel, Andy Youill, Angus McDonald, Archie Johnson, Ariel Wiess, Arta Alho, Arthur Motye, Barrette, C. S. Feslier, C. Villeyea, Captain Thomas Dunbar, Charles E Adams, Charles Villagracia, Charlie Ross, D. M. MacQueen and wife, Dalby, Dennis Roberts, Desire Bourdon, Didelo Diepro, E. Sherrien, Edward Cullen, Edward Sinclair, Eric Ryerson, Flanerty Crawford, Frank Bryon, Fred Bidgood, Fred Clarke, Fred Hamilton, Fred Herbert, Fritz Manse, George Payette, George Snowden Andréws, Harry Brookins, Harry Bruce, Harry Darce or Dance, Harry Hardy, Henry Robert, Herbert Bentley, Howard Genchon, Hugh McLeod, Hugh Meehan, Hugh O'Donnell, J. Coyne, J. J. Shea, J. Moss, J. Paulin, J.W.
                               (MORE)

                    VOICE OVER (cont'd)
Cranshaw, J.Orr , James Rennie, James Sweeney, Jeanna Weiss, John Bilo, John Bowers, John Destern, John McDonald, John McKay, John McLaughlin, John Murray, John S Dekker, John Saunch, John Wall, John Whatmaugh, Joseph Fletcher, Joseph Flynn, Jules Metayer, Lacroix, Lee H. Sulman, Lester Henninger, Mack Smith, Malcom Black, Melvin Strain, Micheal Johnson, Micheal Morrison, Micheal O'Neill, Morris Moffit, Murray, Nathan Haas, O. Jelly, O. Morrison, Ormand (Oscar) Butler, Orpila Mondoux, Oscar Patrice, Patrick Dwyer, R. A. Dwyer, R. J. Welch, Robert Weiss, Roy Brady and companion, Russell Dale, Samuel Brown, Samuel Jeveraux, Stanley Fitzmaage, Stanley Nicholson, Sylvia Hortell, T. A. Dobbins, T. Condil, T. Gravelle, T.R. Geddes, T.W.C. Hutchins, Thomas Bascom, Thomas Bodin, Thomas Cooper, Thomas Croon, Thomas John King, Thomas McLeod, Timothy Robinson, Victor Puera, W. Beeita, William Anthony Thompson, William Black, William Gore (or Gohr), William King, William Mogridge, William Moore, William O'Flynn, William Taylor, William Thackeray

45 **EXT. BURNT GOLDFIELD - SONG AFTER THE FIRE**

                            The chorus assembles for a funeral service. Pastor
                            Schwidder officiates.

                            Pastor Schwidder sings the funeral oration:

                    PASTOR SCHWIDDER
DUST WE ARE AND TO DUST WE SHALL RETURN.
WHAT IS SOWN PERISHABLE; IS RAISED IMPERISHABLE.
SO IT IS WITH THE RESURRECTION OF THE DEAD.

                            ALL
SO IT IS WITH THE RESURRECTION OF THE DEAD.

                            Pearl meets up with her father again.

                            PEARL
Papa!

                            Mr.O'Day embraces his family.

                    PASTOR SCHWIDDER
BEHOLD! I TELL YOU A MYSTERY.
WE SHALL NOT SLEEP, BUT WE SHALL ALL BE CHANGED.
IN A MOMENT, IN THE TWINKLING OF AN EYE,

> Lillian passes a new born baby to her mother.

ALL
AT THE LAST TRUMPET.

> John Gauley goes back to the mine shaft. He looks down then sits sadly at the mouth of the mine. They are all dead. He sings and it mixes with the service that Pastor Schwidder is doing.

JOHN GUALEY
GONE, THEY ARE ALL GONE.
ALL HOPE AND EVERY CARE
LAID IN THE GROUND SO BARE.
GONE, THEY ARE ALL GONE.
LET THE WORLD BE LOST AND STRANGE.
DON'T LET ME SEE THE CHANGE.

IS THERE HOPE THEN IF WE DIE?
CAN MAN STOP DEATH THOUGH HE TRY?
HOW CAN I CARRY ON?
NOW THAT EVERYTHING AROUND ME IS GONE?

PASTOR SCHWIDDER
IN THE MIDST OF LIFE WE ARE IN DEATH.
WHETHER WE LIVE THEREFORE OR DIE, WE ARE THE LORD'S.
NO MAN LIVES TO HIMSELF,
NO MAN DIES TO HIMSELF.

> Will and Christie find each other. Pearl and John find each other.

ALL
SO IT IS WITH THE RESURRECTION OF THE DEAD.

ALL AND JOHN GUALEY
I WILL NOT FORGET.
YOU ARE ON MY MIND.
I WILL REACH FOR YOU ALWAYS,
TIME RUNNING ON FOREVER.

IN MY HEART,
WITH MY EYES,
EVERY PART,
FOREVER.

       ALL AND JOHN GUALEY, PASTOR
       SCHWIDDER
KNOW WHAT YOU HAVE SOWN
WILL RISE IN SMOKE AND ASHES.
SKIES MAY FILL WITH TEARS
WHILE DARKNESS FALLS AND CRASHES.

ALL THESE THINGS MAY CHANGE
I'LL STILL HOLD YOUR NAME.
IN MY HEART,
IN MY EYES,
EVERY PART,
FOREVER.

       PASTOR SCHWIDDER
WE SHALL NOT SLEEP BUT WE SHALL ALL BE CHANGED.

       Caroline exits, looking for André.

       ALL
SO IT IS WITH THE RESURRECTION OF THE DEAD.

       The townspeople gather together in small groups, and walk off.

46 **EXT. BURNT GOLDFIELD - CAROLINE FINDS ANDRÉ - SONG**

       Caroline is back at the plot. There is no sign of André. The plot has been razed clean by the fire, it smokes still. She sings a little of their love song. She sadly kneels on the ground, crying.

       CAROLINE
TES PENSEES ME SONT CHERES,
MON COEUR RESSENT TA JOIE.
J'ENTENDS LA DOUCE TENDRESSE.
MON COUER VIENT VERS...

> André enters singing where she left off. Caroline turns amazed towards him, not sure if it is really him or not. She runs into his arms.

ANDRÉ
SPEAK YOUR WORDS TO ME,
MY HEART KNOWS THEM WELL.
I HEAR EVERY THOUGHT,
YOUR WORDS MEAN TO TELL.

ANDRÉ AND CAROLINE
WHEN YOU SPEAK YOUR WORDS TO ME,
FOR MY HEART WILL LISTEN WELL.

CAROLINE
André! I thought you were dead.

ANDRÉ
I thought I was too, for a while.

CAROLINE
That explosion was so big, I was sure it was the dynamite car.

ANDRÉ
It was. We were able to move it a little way down the track but the fire was coming in too quickly, we only just managed to get cover. If we had been able to get it a few feet further...

CAROLINE
You did what you could. I am glad you're still alive.

ANDRÉ
Look, there's the end of your stake, still in the ground.

CAROLINE
That's amazing, the fire burned around it. Ha, you'd think that someone was having a campfire.

> They look at each other and smile weakly, acknowledging the horror of those words.

CAROLINE (cont'd)
Everything is gone. The trees, the grass, the entrance to the trail, everything.

André brushes aside some of her hair which has come loose.

ANDRÉ
Your hair is loose.

CAROLINE
I'll fix it.

She reaches up to fix her hair.

ANDRÉ
I don't mind.

She lets her hair hang loose. André touches a dirty mark on her face.

André (cont'd)
You have soot on your face.

CAROLINE
Oh, I didn't even realize. My skin is so tight it feels like it has been sunburnt.

ANDRÉ
Je m'excuse. I didn't mean to hurt you.

CAROLINE
I don't mind.

ANDRÉ
Caroline, do you remember when I said you didn't belong here, that you weren't strong enough?

CAROLINE
Yes.

ANDRÉ
I was wrong. You belong here, with me.

They sing.

47   **EXT. BURNT GOLDFIELD - LOVE SONG REPRISE INTO ENDING**

ANDRÉ
EVERYONE HOPES TO FIND THEIR FUTURE
DIGGING DEEP IN HILLS OF GOLD.

THEY HOPE TO FIND THE ANSWER
IN WHAT IS BOUGHT AND SOLD.

          ANDRÉ AND CAROLINE
I WISH EVERY MOMENT
BRINGS LIFE WITH YOU TO SHARE
I'D TRADE THOSE GOLDEN HILLSIDES
TO FIND YOU WAITING THERE.
TIME MAY CHANGE OUR LIVES COMPLETELY
CLOSING EVERY OPEN DOOR.
BRING ON EVERY CHANGING MOMENT
LOVE, I WOULD NOT ASK FOR MORE.

> After a moment, Caroline turns and looks at the ground, it has turned golden.

          CAROLINE
Look! André!

          ANDRÉ
What?

          CAROLINE
Do you see what the fire did? Look at the rock.

          ANDRÉ
It's all bare, every ounce of it.

          CAROLINE
Is that what I think it is?

          ANDRÉ
It's a vein alright. Quartz, shot with flecks of gold.

          CAROLINE
Who won the bet?

          ANDRÉ
I did. I found you first.

          ANDRÉ AND CAROLINE
I WISH EVERY MOMENT
BRINGS LIFE WITH YOU TO SHARE
I'D TRADE THOSE GOLDEN HILLSIDES
TO FIND YOU WAITING THERE.

> The scene stretches out with some of the main characters joining together with their dramatic partners until finally the stage is full. It glows like the golden heart they have finally found. Love and Gold themes join to make one.

                ALL
TIME MAY CHANGE OUR LIVES COMPLETELY
CLOSING EVERY OPEN DOOR.
BRING ON EVERY CHANGING MOMENT
LOVE, I WOULD NOT ASK FOR MORE.

> Maggie carries one of the children she rescued giving the child to her mother. Maggie is about to turn away on her own. Pearl goes to Maggie, taking her hand. Mrs.O'Day joins her.

                PEARL
Don't go Maggie.

                Mrs.O'DAY
We were about to have supper. All we have are some biscuits made with Seldez powder but...

> Maggie tries to politely refuse.

                MAGGIE
I wouldn't want to be any trouble.

                MRS.O'DAY
It would be our pleasure Maggie. We would be honored.

                MAGGIE
Alright then.

> Maggie smiles as she exits with the O'Day family, Pearl holding her hand.
>
> Will and Christy are looking through the remains of their burnt house together. André and Caroline, who have just arrived, watch with sympathy. Will moves the charred wood with his foot. Clearing the area he speaks sadly.

                WILL
Gold.

> André looks at Caroline. Caroline collects a few tools while André walks over to Will carrying what will be the start of a new house. As he sings, he helps Will begin rebuilding his house.

ANDRÉ
OUR ARMS KNOW THE GREATEST OF RICHES.

> Caroline joins in, helping to build.

ANDRÉ AND CAROLINE
OUR HEARTS KNOW THEIR LIBERTY.

> Christie joins in, encouraging Will.

ANDRÉ AND CAROLINE AND CHRISTY
WE ALL KNOW THE LIFE THAT WE LOOKED FOR,
LIES ALL AROUND US NOT UNDER OUR FEET.

48 **EXT. BURNT PORCUPINE CAMP -THE CULTURES UNITE - SONG**

> One by one families bring tools and wood to help. Starting with the French. The leader sets his wood purposefully on the corner of the "foundation." He looks a grateful Will in the eye as his family gathers around him.
>
> Each group comes forward quickly (in the order they arrived in at the beginning) and the frame of the house begins to appear. As they drive in their wood they each declare the word "gold" in their language. The word has taken on new meaning, it is the gold that they have found in each other that is worth saving.
>
> John and Pearl, followed by the remaining children, arrive with hammers and tools. The children thrust the tools triumphantly into the air as everyone cries...

ALL
OR, OR ... KULTA, KULTA ... ZOLOTO, ZOLOTO ... GOLD, GOLD.
YOU ARE MY GOLD.

THOUGH TIME MUST CLOSE MOST EVERY DOOR.
I HOPE TO LIVE AND NEVER ASK MORE.

I CAN'T CHANGE THE PAST BUT I PROMISE
YOURS IS THE HEART THAT MY HEART WILL ADORE.

PLEASE TAKE MY HAND I'LL WALK WITH YOU NOW.
BRING NIGHT OR DAY I'LL KEEP TO MY VOW.
YOU AND I WILL BUILD FOR EACH OTHER
HOMES FULL OF HOPE THAT OUR HEARTS CAN ENDOW.

MY ARMS, THEY KNOW OF RICHES MOST SWEET.
OUR HEARTS THEY THEIR LIBERTY.
WE ALL KNOW THE LIFE THAT WE LOOKED FOR,
LIES ALL AROUND US NOT UNDER OUR FEET.

YOU ARE MY GOLD!

49 **EXT. GOLDFIELD/MEMORY WORLD - WE ARE HOME - SONG**

Will and Christie's new house has been built. The Porcupine camp is now united. As Caroline and André go off together to build a new life, the people of the camp sing.

ALL
WHEN YOUR FEET ARE LOST AND WEARY,
THERE'S A LIGHT TO LEAD YOU HOME.
WHEN YOUR EYES WILL NOT SEE CLEARLY,
THIS SURE LIGHT WILL LEAD YOU HOME.

COME ON HOME.
OUR HANDS WILL BUILD TOGETHER,
STAY STRONG, WE WILL REMEMBER,
WE ARE HOME,
THIS IS HOME!

WHEN THE HOPE YOU HAVE IS SCATTERED.
AND THE WORLD YOU KNEW IS LOST.
THINK OF THOSE YOU KNEW WHO MATTERED.
DON'T LOOK BACK FOR WHAT IT COST.

COME ON HOME.
LOVE WILL LEAD YOU BLINDLY.
COME ON HOME.
CLING TO IT THOUGH TIGHTLY.
IT WILL LEAD,
LEAD YOU HOME!

At the time of the fire, our house had just been built, we had just nicely moved in there. Yes, the wind had been blowing pretty hard. There had been a long, dry spell and Mother and Dad had talked several times about; they just hoped everybody would be careful of campfires and that sort of thing, because the timber was so dry. We were doing chores around the house, and Dad came rushing and told to get to the water as soon as we could, to get down to the creek. So we got down and he said he'd see us later

DURING PORCUPINE FIRE AT GOLDEN CITY.

FIRE IN PORCUPINE JULY 11/11   H. PETERS PHOTO

GETTING MAIL AFTER FIRE SOUTH PORCUPINE

Glossary

French Phrases

Bon ami – *good friend*
Donne-moi la main. – *Give me your hand*
Ça tourne pas rond la dedans! – (Rough Translation) *Are you crazy? (Is nothing turning round in your head?)*
Quels beaux cheveux, Minnie… Comme la crinière d'un cheval. – *What beautiful hair… just like a horse's mane.*
Un cheval qui se lave… et… se brosse… – *A horse that washes… and brushes…*
Salut – *Hello*
J'ai entendu dire! – *You are telling me!*
Fais moi pas rire! – *Don't make me laugh!*
Quoi dire? – *What can I say?*
Tout seul n'est-ce pas? – *Always (Completely) alone, yes?*
Quoi? – *What?*
Pas elle! – *Not her!*
Ce n'est pas bon – *that's not good*
Allons-y! – *Let's go!*
Le Théâtre des Champs-Élysées est sans conteste l'un des plus beaux lieux de spectacle parisiens - *The Champs-Élysées Theatre is without question the most beautiful concert hall in Paris.*
Vous avez besoin de quelqu'un pour vous aider. – *You need someone to help you.*
Ce serait mon plaisir Madamoiselle – *This would be my pleasure, Madamoiselle.*
sous la toile des étoiles scintillantes– *under the weaving of bright stars*
Pour nos deux, un spectacle d'amoureux– *For the two of us, a show of love*
Sous la lune tout près de moi – *Under the moon, always next to me.*
Dans mon coeur, le destin de mes rêves – *in my heart, the destiny of all my dreams*
Si je t'ouvre la porte de mon coeur– *If I open the door of my heart to you*
Dans mon Coeur, je veux te reconter - *in my heart I want to meet you*
Dans la joie, je serai près de toi- *in joy I will always be next to you*
Bêtise – *stupid, bad mistake*
Es-tu Fou! – *Are you crazy?*

Finnish Phrases

Kulta– *gold*
Minun kotimaa, kaunis suomi - *My homeland, Beautiful Finland*
Suomissa on järviä ja jokia - *In Finland there are lakes and rivers*
Toivoton nahda teidat kesalla kun kukat kuki - *I hope to see you in the summer when the flowers bloom*
Tuon kaiki kullan mitä voin kantta - *I will bring you all the gold I can carry*
Kun pääsen kotia en lahden enää pois - *When I get home I won't ever leave again.*

Ukrainian Phrases

Koli Ya Preydu Dodohmoo – *When I return home*
Mi zoostrinemo Na Poleev - *we will meet in the feilds*
Tehploh Nasha Seemya Mi Budehmoh Znahti Znohvoo - *We will know warmth with our family again*
Slava Ucryeena, Moiee Brati! - *Praise Ukraine, my brothers!*
Nashi Prekrasnoo Poleev Zjivi Eez Zohlohteh Zerno! - *Our dear fields alive with golden grain!*
Tahntsaueay, Moi Sehstri! - *Dance again my sisters!*
Mi Boodehmoh Znahti Bahhotstvo Znohvoo! - *We will know riches again!*

Scottish Phrases

Hald – *held, to hold, to keep*
Sough - *sigh*
Clunk - *to make a hollow sound*
Jillet - *jilt (to be jilted, thrown over)*
Laird - *Lord (land owner)*
Auld - *old*
Sair - *serve*
Guid - *good*
Gree - *prize*
Ha'folk - *servants*
Haddin - *inheritance, holding*
Clink - *money*
Cog - *drinking bowl*

Ojibway Phrases

Zeebeh gee kendahn – *The River Knows*
Gawenishekay gahzee – *You are not alone*
Tza gee gowah – *You are surrounded by love*

Irish Phrases

With the Elephant – *Drinking (getting drunk)*
Cuttie – *young girl*

Weird Words

"Blind Pig" – *Back in the early mining days it was illegal for anyone to sell alcohol within a certain number of miles of the mine. It was hoped miners would go home with their money instead of spending it on drink. Of course, many establishments were more than willing to fill the illegal gap, in this case, the drug store (which also served food in those days.) Fact: In the Porcupine Camp there was also an establishment called the "White Rat" that ran a "green house." People looking for a drink would pop in for "flowers and vegetables!"*

"Stakes and Claims"- *Things prospectors knew: how to follow the compass and stars, how to carry large packs into the woods, and how to find lots of adventure. They often had no formal training, only luck and hunches. They did know how to look for rocky outcrops with a vein (an up thrust of mineral). They could mark out a forty acre claim with a "twenty chains" or 1320 foot side. They only had a number of permissible claims per year, and that is one reason they often worked in groups. In Canada a person was free to stake a claim for themselves. They rarely patented their own claims. Patenting required forty days of work a year, over five years. Most prospectors had no interest in becoming a manager, they simply wanted to claim as much as they could, as quickly as possible.*

"Put Him through the Ringer" – *A ringer was an old fashioned dryer that literally squeezed the fabric between two cylinders to get the water out. Actually putting someone through the ringer would be impossible, but my guess is, Minnie would still try!*

oil of cajeput – *1900's antiseptic for wounds.*

Performer's Notes

Laureen Kuhl – Book, Lyrics, Melodies

Born in Toronto and raised in Owen Sound, Laureen began performing in musicals at the tender age of seven. By the time she was fifteen she was directing and writing for the public on a regular basis. She went on to receive her Bachelor of Arts from York University's Theatre Program where she also completed the three-year screenwriting program. She has since worked as a director, writer, and performer in theatre troupes throughout Ontario and in the UK. Her writing has won awards for both playwriting and poetry. Recent productions of her written work include, "Ye Olde Christmas Variety Showe," and "The Pirates of Penzance: Adapted," for the *Timmins Symphony Orchestra*, "The Pond," for the *Kitchener Waterloo Little Theatre*, and a series of sketches called "The Treasure Chest" which saw touring productions across Canada. Laureen also works as a freelance writer and is currently working towards publishing a poetry book: "Hope Springs, Hope Clings: Poems for Hope and Love in the World" as well as a short story, "The Architect's Tower."

Laureen is the proud mother of four little citizens of Timmins, and is thrilled to be able to tell them the story of the Porcupine Camp, an important part of Canadian history that occurred right in their own backyard.

Luc Martin – Music, Melodies and Orchestration

Born in Alexandria, Ontario, Luc studied composition at the University of Ottawa where he graduated with a Masters in Music in 2004. Under the tutelage of Steven Gellman and John Armstrong, Luc developed, a style of composition that is unique and yet accessible. Luc's main musical influences are Beethoven, Shostakovich and the impressionist composers of the early 20th century.

Now residing in Timmins Ontario, Luc spends most of his free time working on various composition projects. In addition to the composition of the *Heart of Gold* musical, he is presently working on a series of piano preludes and a multi-movement work for oboe d'amore and string quartet. Most recently he has completed the composition of the single movement work *Petits oiseaux bleus* for cello and flute.

Luc's works have been performed throughout Canada. The Ottawa Chamber Music Society has premiered several works including *Fugue (2004) and Scherzo (2005)*. The Kanata Symphony Orchestra premiered Luc's first piano concerto in 2004. More recently, The Xstrata String Quartet premiered *Trio #1* during its 2009-2010 chamber series. The Timmins Symphony Orchestra premiered the multi-movement orchestral work *Metempsychose III, À la mémoire d'Amélie Guertin* during the opening concert of the 2010 main concert series.

www.ingramcontent.com/pod-product-compliance
Lightning Source LLC
Chambersburg PA
CBHW080342170426
43194CB00014B/2659